NO-WASTE
Composting

Small-Space Waste Recycling, Indoors and Out

Michelle Balz

COOL
SPRINGS
PRESS

Brimming with creative inspiration, how-to projects, and useful information to enrich your everyday life, Quarto Knows is a favorite destination for those pursuing their interests and passions. Visit our site and dig deeper with our books into your area of interest: Quarto Creates, Quarto Cooks, Quarto Homes, Quarto Lives, Quarto Drives, Quarto Explores, Quarto Gifts, or Quarto Kids.

© 2021 Quarto Publishing Group USA Inc.
Text © 2021 Michelle Balz

First Published in 2021 by Cool Springs Press,
an imprint of The Quarto Group,
100 Cummings Center, Suite 265-D,
Beverly, MA 01915, USA.
T (978) 282-9590 F (978) 283-2742 QuartoKnows.com

Cool Springs Press titles are also available at discount
for retail, wholesale, promotional, and bulk purchase.
For details, contact the Special Sales Manager by email
at specialsales@quarto.com or by mail at The Quarto
Group, Attn: Special Sales Manager, 100 Cummings
Center, Suite 265-D, Beverly, MA 01915, USA.

25 24 23 22 21   1 2 3 4 5

ISBN: 978-0-7603-6870-1

Digital edition published in 2021
eISBN: 978-0-7603-6871-8

Library of Congress Cataloging-in-Publication Data
available

Cover Design: The Quarto Group
Page Design and Layout: Laura Shaw Design
Photography by Andrea MacFarland except as follows:
Kathy Kugler, page 71 (right); Anna Stockton, pages 31
(right), 61, 83 (left), and 86–88.
Illustration: Mattie Wells
Bin Design and Construction: Adam Balz

Printed in China

For my children, Ben and Emily, and all of
my nieces and nephews, Josie, Ava, Heidi,
Violet, John, Elena, and Archer.

Be a force in the world for kindness,
regeneration, and hope.

CONTENTS

|||||||||||||||||||||||||||||||||||||||||

INTRODUCTION

Once you start successfully home composting it becomes so much more than just another habit. It becomes an obsession. You are not simply someone who composts. You become a composter. Something about transforming old banana peels, dead leaves, and coffee grounds—stuff many people consider "garbage"—into the most beautiful, rich, crumbly soil amendment transforms you as well. You become more self-sufficient, more capable, and more connected to the world under your feet.

This book contains more than a dozen simple DIY projects to create your own backyard or in-home composting system using reused and repurposed materials. Many of the projects use items you or your friends already have on hand. That means you can start home composting without shelling out any, or at least very little, money.

Already have a compost bin? Great! This book also provides you with all of the knowledge you need to become a composter. So often people start composting only to stop because they don't know the few basic rules to follow. Chapter 2 lays out how to balance browns and greens, what you can and cannot compost, and how to maintain your compost pile with very little work.

Of course, knowing the rules and knowing when to break them makes life more interesting, so I've included a few innovative composting methods for those of you who want to compost indoors, on your patio, or in your garden without a bin at all. You will also learn special techniques for composting materials traditionally left out of home composting, such as meat and dog poop. Yes, I have a whole chapter for composting Fido's manure. You're welcome.

Whether you already compost and want to step up your composting game or you are just starting your composting journey, this book will help you become a successful backyard composter. Transform your garbage into gardener's gold. Build your own composting system using repurposed materials. Become more self-sufficient and resourceful.

Well, composter, are you obsessed yet?

▶ This book includes many simple DIY projects to create your own in-home or backyard composting system, including the Repurposed Trash Can Tumbler in chapter 3.

◀ Transform old banana peels, apple cores, and dead leaves into a valuable soil amendment for your garden.

No—Waste Lifestyle and Benefits of Composting

IIIIIIIIIIIIIIIIIIIIIIIIIIIIIIIIIIIIIIIIIIII

NO—WASTE LIFESTYLE

When you think about how much garbage we create in our everyday lives, living a no-waste or zero-waste lifestyle may seem impossible, but hear me out. I see living with no waste as an aspirational goal: I take small steps, making changes in the products I buy and what I do with materials once their useful life with me is over. Striving toward zero waste just means you are trying to use our natural resources in the most efficient and smartest way possible, so we can conserve and preserve the planet we all love. Incorporating composting into your life gives you a huge leap toward living with no waste.

Reuse provides another leap toward no waste. In the 3R hierarchy you may have learned about in elementary school—reduce, reuse, recycle—reuse ranks higher than recycling as having a stronger environmental impact because it uses fewer resources. Composting technically falls into the "recycling" definition because we (or, rather, our microbe friends) transform one material into something new.

You can jump on the reuse bandwagon in multiple ways, and this book is full of reuse projects. Intentionally reusing everyday products and packaging appeals to the frugal, penny-pinching aspect of our personalities and to our inner environmentalists. Consider shopping for your lumber and other supplies at a building materials reuse center. These are like thrift stores for building supplies, and you can have a lot of fun just walking through the place and discovering treasures. Reuse surplus materials you have lying around your house and garage to construct the bins featured in this book. Instead of purchasing a fancy new kitchen collector,

This composter made from an old pickle barrel resembles something you would buy online, but it only cost a few dollars to make.

just use an old butter tub or coffee canister. Give the item a facelift by printing a list of what you can compost on a durable sticker for the outside.

You can also get creative in the sourcing of your supplies. A friend of mine found the second hand pickle barrel we used to make the composter in chapter 3 (page 43) far cheaper than you would find a new one online. It even smelled like mouth watering pickles. Sometimes manufacturers and stores have leftover pallets that are perfect for making the salvaged pallet bin in chapter 3 (page 46). Have any friends who work in restaurants? They may have access to 5-gallon (19-L) buckets for the pet septic project in chapter 6 (page 106).

Take one step toward no waste and then another—before you know it, you'll be pushing a much lighter trash can to the curb each week.

BUILDING REUSE CENTERS

Building material reuse centers offer used building supplies such as lumber and fixtures at a discounted price.

These used shutters could see a second life as a compost bin.

Whenever I try to explain to a friend what a building reuse center is, I always end up saying, "It's like a thrift store, but for building supplies such as lumber and appliances." You really can't understand until you visit one and experience the wonder and glory for yourself. I am like a kid in a candy shop in these places. It also helps that I love old stuff and could spend hours just admiring the antique doorknobs, ornate fireplace mantels, and unique light fixtures.

Some stores can become a bit unorganized at times, and you may have to clean up your purchases before they reach their true splendor. The money you save and the natural resources you conserve are worth the extra effort. I encourage you to visit a few different reuse stores if they are available in your area because they often specialize in certain materials.

Compost improves the soil to make your garden thrive.

BENEFITS OF COMPOSTING

Imagine taking materials that many people view as garbage and transforming them into something useful. When you compost, you create something that will amend your soil and improve your garden. You create something that has the ability to bind heavy metals so your plants won't absorb them. You create something that reduces your need for fertilizers and pesticides. Best of all, creating this special something requires no electricity, and you can make all the tools you need yourself.

Compost holds a special place in the hearts of serious gardeners as the most important soil amendment around. But aside from the many personal benefits you reap from composting, your decision to compost also benefits the world around you, positively affecting larger environmental issues. You win, your soil wins, and the planet wins.

FEEDING THE SOIL

Plants need sixteen essential chemical elements for growth. Compost helps your plants obtain these nutrients in two ways.

First, compost contains many of these nutrients because the material you added—leaves, food scraps, coffee grounds, and more—contained these nutrients. As the material breaks down in your compost, many of these nutrients become available for plant consumption.

Second, and arguably more important, compost improves the living area of the soil for beneficial microorganisms so they grow, reproduce, and prosper. These tiny organisms in the soil make the nutrients available to your plants and pull minerals from the surrounding soil to feed your plants.

Compost is not fertilizer. People design fertilizer to feed plants. Compost feeds the soil. This distinction may seem minor, but soil is not a barren lifeless matter—it's a whole ecosystem teeming with life. The compost we add improves the life in the soil, thereby helping to nourish the plants.

INCREASING SOIL AERATION

Amending your soil with compost improves the soil tilth, or health of the soil as it relates to plants. If you have heavy clay soils, compost breaks apart the tight structure, making the soil more friable for better aeration and drainage. Plant roots have an easier time growing in the amended soil, and the varied structure of the compost will hold small pockets of air for both the roots and the organisms living in the soil. The gift that keeps on giving, compost also creates a soil habitat where macroinvertebrates thrive. Those little creatures moving around in the soil will continue to keep the soil aerated into the future.

PREVENTING EROSION

When raindrops hit bare soil, they have so much energy they can blow apart particles on the surface of the soil. The wet soil particles then separate by size and density, creating layers as they settle, with the finest soil particles settling on top. This process forms a crust on the soil that prevents water from penetrating to the lower layers of soil (and your plants' roots). The newly formed crust also becomes prone to cracking where the streams of water form while running off. Soil cracking and crust creation begin the process of soil erosion and degradation. A nice layer of compost on the top of the soil cushions the falling raindrops, absorbing the energy and protecting the soil underneath.

The large amount of organic matter in compost also acts like a bonding agent in the soil structure. The compost holds the soil in place against rain and wind. When you place compost on a sloped area, it reduces the soil's natural inclination to slide down the hill. Engineers, farmers, and soil conservationists all recognize this benefit and use compost on sites susceptible to soil erosion. Tap into this compost superpower and apply compost to areas where erosion may pull away your soil.

IMPROVING YOUR SOIL

Amending your soil with compost is one of the most important actions you can take to improve and preserve soil in your garden. If traditional farmers had easier access to large amounts of compost, you would see them using this miracle amendment more often. The good news is that we have the power to make compost in our own backyards. We generate raw compostable materials every day in our kitchens and gardens. Because we work on a smaller scale as individuals, creating compost happens naturally and easily. We only need to seize the opportunity to create this amazing soil amendment.

ENVIRONMENTAL BENEFITS

You may have heard the saying "think global, act local." Backyard composting embraces this philosophy. Setting aside materials from our trash to create a resource for our own backyard can positively affect the environment on a global scale. Sometimes it is hard to imagine that one person can make a difference to something as large as our planet, but imagine the impact if everyone in your neighborhood or your city started composting in their backyards. What we do matters.

clockwise from upper left **Compost tumblers require a little more work but will create finished compost more quickly. Feed your landscape, not the landfill, by composting food scraps at home. Reducing our waste conserves resources for future generations. Amending your soil with compost improves soil aeration and tilth, making plants happy to call it home.**

FEEDING YOUR LANDSCAPE, NOT THE LANDFILL

Compostable yard trimmings, food waste, and paper could make up between one-third and one-half of your garbage. In the United States, about 30 percent of the garbage a household creates could easily be composted in the backyard (about 1,234 pounds, or 560 kg, per year). This doesn't include the newspaper and cardboard that we could compost but generally recycle.

By composting the material in your backyard, your compostables do not take up space in the garbage truck. The truck will pick up more houses per trip, reducing the fuel needed to collect the route. Your materials also do not take up space at the landfill, extending the life of that landfill and delaying the need to build another. Composting means you put less waste at the curb, leading to lighter garbage and yard waste trucks, longer life at the landfill, and smiles all around.

ACT TO PREVENT WASTED FOOD

Save edible food scraps in a bag in your freezer to create vegetable broth before the veggies go to the compost.

Setting aside food scraps for composting in your backyard makes you keenly aware of how much food you waste. Some things, such as banana peels and melon rinds, are unavoidable. Others, such as the slimy zucchini forgotten in the back of the produce drawer and the moldy strawberries we meant to eat, could have been avoided. Bringing the inedible food that had so much potential back to the compost pile for a productive burial doesn't seem like enough.

Each bite of food we eat tells a story, from the labor of the farmer to the soil and water used to grow the food, the fuel to transport the food, and the energy to keep the food fresh in the store and your home. Our food requires so many resources. Composting what we waste is certainly better than just sending it to the landfill, but we can take a few steps to reduce wasted food in our households (and save money at the same time).

▶ **GROCERY SHOP WITH INTENTION.** Take stock of your pantry and refrigerator. Plan meals ahead to use up foods before they go bad. Create a grocery list and stick to the list as best you can.

▶ **MAKE USE OF YOUR FREEZER.** This impressive appliance helps you preserve your food to eat another day. Prepared foods make easy meals when you don't feel like cooking. Peel bananas past their prime and freeze the fruit for later use in delicious smoothies.

▶ **REVIVE YOUR FOOD.** Revive bendy carrots and wilted lettuce by placing them in an ice-water bath for 5 to 10 minutes. Toast stale bread and crackers in the oven for a few minutes. Blend overcooked veggies into a sauce or soup.

▶ **CREATE A BROTH BAG IN YOUR FREEZER.** You can put almost any unused vegetable in this bag. When a recipe calls for half an onion, place the unused half in the freezer bag. When you only need mushroom caps, place the stems in the freezer bag. Toss kale ribs and stems into the bag. Then, create a stock by simmering the vegetables in water for 30 minutes or until they are well cooked. Strain and use the broth to make a soup or freeze it for later. Add all those mushy vegetables to your compost pile. They will decompose with dignity, knowing you squeezed every penny out of that produce.

REDUCE YOUR CARBON FOOTPRINT

Backyard composting reduces your carbon footprint, or the amount of greenhouse gases that living your life generates. When plants decompose, they naturally release the carbon dioxide (CO_2) absorbed during their lives. Plants and food scraps also do this in your compost bin. It's okay; that's what they're supposed to do.

But when buried in the landfill with no air, food and yard waste decompose anaerobically and release methane instead. Methane traps heat in our atmosphere and has an impact twenty-five times greater than CO_2 over a hundred-year period. By encouraging the right kind of decomposition, you reduce the greenhouse-gas impact of your yard trimmings and food scraps and lessen global climate change. Yay for you!

But hold onto your hats because compost has another even more amazing trick up its brown, crumbly sleeve. Adding compost and the microorganisms that come with it to your soil allows soil to amazingly store carbon so it does not become CO_2 in our atmosphere. This starts with plants growing in your fertile soil. Plants pull CO_2 out of the air in the process we all know and love: photosynthesis. What the plant doesn't use during photosynthesis it pulls down to the roots and gives to the organisms in the soil surrounding the roots. Those soil organisms, especially the fungi, use and stabilize the carbon in a form that the soil can store for thousands of years. We call it a "carbon sink" and a trick like that deserves a standing ovation.

Amending your soil with compost allows the soil to store more carbon from the atmosphere, reducing climate change.

Composting Basics

||||||||||||||||||||||||||||||||||||

A QUICK PRIMER

When you plant a garden, you control (or try to control) which plants grow and where they grow. When you compost, you attempt to control what materials decompose and where they decompose. In the process, you create a valuable soil amendment, reduce household waste, and start an avalanche of other personal and environmental benefits.

Home composting can involve a structure or a container, or you can integrate composting directly into your garden. You can put as much or as little effort as you choose into your composting, depending on how quickly you want a finished product. Backyard composting is very forgiving, so even when you make mistakes, you end up with pretty darn good compost.

In nature, there is no waste—everything decomposes and continues in a circle to nourish new life. Humus is the organic component of soil formed by decomposition. Nature takes decades and sometimes centuries to create beautiful, humus-filled topsoil: Trees release leaves that naturally decompose where they fall. Animals contribute manure, regularly adding a rich, nutrient-filled material to the cycle. Decomposers, such as earthworms, help break everything down and slowly build the topsoil year after year.

When you compost in the backyard, you're replicating what happens naturally, but in a concentrated and controlled manner. You're creating that humus material you find on the forest floor. You're just not waiting hundreds of years to get it done.

THE SECRET GOAL OF COMPOSTING

If maintained correctly, your backyard compost bin contains an entire food web with billions of organisms working together to decompose your food scraps into rich, beautiful compost.

First, I'll let you in on a little secret. Everything we do when composting, from constructing the bin to maintaining the pile, is all to keep the micro- and macroorganisms in your bin alive and happy. If you properly maintain your compost, the environment you create becomes the ideal habitat for creatures you can see and creatures you cannot see. These organisms work together, transforming your banana peels into beautiful, crumbly compost. To successfully compost, we need to supply our little friends with the right amount of air, water, and food, and the service they provide is well worth our efforts.

A traditional backyard compost bin creates beautiful finished compost.

MACROORGANISMS: CREATURES YOU CAN SEE

Macroorganisms such as worms, millipedes, and beetles have a role to play in our controlled decomposition. Our favorite macroorganisms, the decomposers, eat bacteria, fungi, rotting vegetables, and leaves. These include worms, millipedes, sow bugs, and springtails. The larvae from beetles and most other creatures also fall in this group. These organisms help break down particles in the pile and contribute manure.

When backyard composting, you do not need to add earthworms (or any other organism) to your pile. If you build it, they will come. Earthworms and other macroorganisms will naturally squirm, crawl, or hop into your pile and accept decaying matter as payment for their invaluable service.

Other macroorganisms, the predatory types such as spiders and centipedes, we tolerate at our composting party because they are part of a healthy food web. These mini lions will naturally eat our favorite decomposer friends, but that is all part of the circle of life (cue music) and not something you need to worry about unless you are vermicomposting (see "Vermicomposting" in chapter 5).

EARTHWORMS

The heavyweight champions of the composting food web, earthworms consume an inspiring amount of material, turning and aerating the pile in the process. Their tunnels allow air, water, and other organisms deeper access to the pile. Mostly one long digestive system, earthworms grind food in their gizzards and use digestive juices to further break the material down. Their casts—worm poop—come out of the worm richer in bacteria, organic matter, and available nitrogen than what went into the worm. Composters love earthworms, and I like to think they return the sentiment.

Earthworms consume a large amount of material, and their tunnels allow air, water, and other organisms access to the compost.

MICROORGANISMS AND FUNGI

For the inhabitants of your compost bin to turn food scraps and dry leaves into rich, luscious compost, you need both physical degradation of the material into smaller pieces and chemical transformation of the material. Bacteria, actinomycetes, protozoa, and fungi perform the necessary chemical decomposition services. While all these organisms play their part, bacteria perform the bulk of the work.

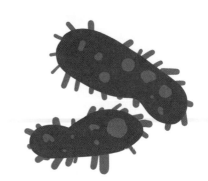

Bacteria

The type of bacteria in your compost bin will vary depending on where you live, what material you put in, the time of year, and how often you turn your pile. Regardless of what you do or do not do, bacteria are there. Bacteria coat every surface of everything in your pile. This is good news for composters because bacteria are among the most adaptable eaters on the planet, able to produce the needed enzymes to digest just about anything you put in front of them.

These microorganisms operate under the "live hard, die young" philosophy, usually only having a lifespan of 20 to 30 minutes. But one single-celled organism can yield a progeny of billions in just a few hours. You may remember from school that a piece of garden soil the size of a pea can contain a billion bacteria.

Fungi

Most types of fungi living in your compost bin are saprophytes, organisms that obtain energy by breaking down organic matter in dead or dying plants and animals—just the kind of decomposer we want in our compost. Although you will occasionally see some fuzzy mold on items kept in your kitchen collector too long, most of fungi's work begins after the pile has heated and cooled in the final stages of composting.

Fungi include molds (moulds) and yeasts, and most of the time, you will not even see they are present. They work as unseen filaments breaking down tough debris the bacteria cannot handle.

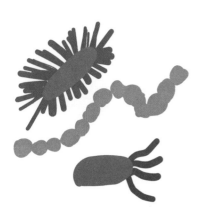

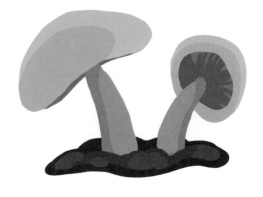

▲ The only material still distinguishable in this small harvest of finished compost are the eggshells.

◀ A lot of action happens in a compost bin without us even seeing our microorganism friends at work.

Actinomycetes

"You smell like actinomycetes" is probably the highest compliment you could bestow on a composter. These organisms are the "earthy" in an earthy scent and give finished compost and freshly plowed earth their signature smell. Similar to fungi but also bacteria, these creatures are critical to making compost. If you see something that looks like spider webs stretching through the first few inches of your pile, you have found colonies of actinomycetes growing in long, threadlike filaments.

Actinomycetes have special enzymes that allow them to break down woody stems and bark. Although some species of this group show up when your pile heats up, like fungi does, they tend to arrive toward the end of the compost process.

WE ARE ALL IN THIS TOGETHER

As a composter, your job is to provide a habitat for these organisms to do their job of decomposition. Your food scraps and brown leaves add fuel to the system. The physical decomposers, such as the worms and the millipedes, grind their way through what you add. The smallest organisms in the pile step in at different stages of decomposition to ultimately transform that apple core into our desired end product.

We provide water for these organisms to survive and air for them to breathe. We protect them from the strongest elements of weather to keep them working around the clock and most of the year. We supply a well-balanced diet of carbon and nitrogen to give our friends the nutrients they need to grow (more on how to do this in a bit). If we succeed in providing the habitat, the macro- and microorganisms will succeed in making finished compost. After you harvest your brown gold, patting your tiny composting friends on the back is optional.

ZEN AND THE ART OF CARBON AND NITROGEN BALANCE

One of the most fundamental skills a backyard composter learns is how to balance "brown" and "green" material. Too many green, or high-nitrogen, items and you will end up with a stinky mess. Too many brown, or high-carbon, items and your pile will decompose slower than a herd of turtles stampeding through peanut butter.

So how do you tell the difference between green and brown? Brown materials are rich in carbon, meaning they have a much higher carbon content compared with nitrogen content. Green materials have a relatively higher percentage of nitrogen than the brown materials. The nitrogen helps speed up the decomposition of the brown materials.

Add about three parts from the brown pile for every one part from the green pile. Don't worry about pulling out the scale or the measuring cups. You gain an intuitive feel for the right balance the more you compost. Remember, composting is forgiving, and these items will break down regardless of how much you add.

Try to balance your compost with three parts brown or high-carbon material (like leaves) to one part green or high-nitrogen material (like food scraps).

Dried leaves form the basis of most backyard composting.

WHAT YOU CAN AND CANNOT COMPOST

At its most basic, what you can compost in your backyard boils down to this question: Did it come from a plant? If the answer is yes, then most likely you can compost it in your backyard. As with all things, there are exceptions to this rule.

Yard Trimmings
This includes anything you rake, cut, pull, and thin from your yard. Leaves, grass, unseeded weeds, excess plants, and anything else narrower than your pinkie finger make excellent compost fodder.

What about the larger branches and woody-stalked plants? You can compost these, but large pieces of wood will take years to decompose. Every year when you harvest, you will have to pull these mildly annoying sticks out from the rest of the compost.

Should you find yourself with a large amount of woody material and a nice sharp shovel, consider the Hügelkultur (pronounced hoo-gul-culture) method of composting described in chapter 4. This integrated method of composting buries woody material under a raised garden bed, allowing the wood to slowly decompose over time.

Kitchen Scraps
This includes anything from a fruit or vegetable. Banana peels, apple cores, and stubs of lettuce all qualify. That slimy zucchini you forgot in the back of the produce drawer? Throw it in the compost! Those lovely grounds from your morning coffee? Yes, please!

Other kitchen scraps derived from plants, such as bread, rice, and crackers, can also go into a compost pile. Cooked and processed scraps are more likely to have butter or oil, which you want to avoid, and breads and grains can create a garbagy smell in your bin if not completely buried.

Always cover your food scraps with leaves, shredded newspaper, or some other "brown" material. This will deter fruit flies and odors.

Locating a leaf bin next to your food scrap composter makes covering food scraps with leaves easier.

Important: Always bury kitchen scraps with a generous layer of leaves. You should not be able to see broccoli stems or banana peels peeking out when you look into your pile. Burying your food scraps will eliminate odors and pesky fruit flies.

Herbivore Manure

Manure and bedding from animals that only eat plants make excellent additions to your compost pile. For the typical backyard composter, these animals include rabbits, gerbils, hamsters, and mice. Most domestic birds also create manure that you can easily compost in your backyard.

Aside from animals you keep as pets inside your home, you may have access to manure from farmed animals such as horses, cows, and goats. The high nitrogen content of all herbivore manure makes an excellent addition to your backyard compost, especially in the integrated composting techniques described in chapter 4. A small amount of this high-nitrogen material will go a long way in a contained compost bin.

STUFF YOU CAN COMPOST

High-Carbon "Brown"

▶ Brown leaves
▶ Dead plants and flowers
▶ Straw
▶ Pine needles
▶ Sawdust and wood chips
▶ Shredded newspaper
▶ Small pieces of brush and shrubs
▶ Cornstalks and husks

High-Nitrogen "Green"

▶ Fruit scraps
▶ Vegetable scraps
▶ Bread, crackers, and pasta
▶ Coffee grounds and filters
▶ Loose tea and tea bags
▶ Green grass
▶ Green plants
▶ Manure from herbivores

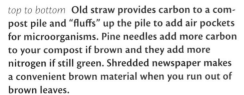

top to bottom **Old straw provides carbon to a compost pile and "fluffs" up the pile to add air pockets for microorganisms. Pine needles add more carbon to your compost if brown and they add more nitrogen if still green. Shredded newspaper makes a convenient brown material when you run out of brown leaves.**

top to bottom **Coffee grounds add a boost of nitrogen to your compost and while they smell great to us, the coffee deters animals. Either leave mowed grass on your lawn to fertilize in place or rake up the cut grass to add to your compost.**

STUFF YOU SHOULDN'T COMPOST

Putting the wrong materials into your compost can cause garbagy odors, attract pests such as flies or rodents, and even cause a health risk. Here is a list of what you should not put in your bin:

- Meat and dairy products (see "Bokashi" in chapter 5)
- Fish or fish parts
- Bones
- Grease, oil, and fat

- Charcoal ash or briquettes
- Diseased plants
- Weed seeds
- Dog or cat manure (see chapter 6)

COMPOSTING WEEDS AND INVASIVE PLANTS

Composting weeds is a matter of personal preference. I say the more the merrier when it comes to adding material to the compost bin. My philosophy is that those dandelion puffballs spread seeds through the air no matter how meticulously I try to avoid them. Why not throw your harvested weeds into the compost to reap the benefits of all that nitrogen?

But I know some composters who dutifully separate out weeds with seeds from other yard trimmings so the seeds will not end up in their finished compost. You cannot guarantee that those seeds will get hot enough to decompose completely in the pile. As you spread your finished compost, you could also be spreading weed seeds (now in the perfect growing medium). To me, it is a risk worth taking, but you will have to decide for yourself.

A few invasive plants (depending on where you live) will not die in your compost pile, and I recommend you do not include those for nature's sake. Check with your local agricultural extension office for a list of the invasive plants in your area.

Dandelions and other weeds provide nitrogen for my compost. You can decide whether its worth the risk of their seeds ending up in your compost.

UNTRADITIONAL COMPOSTABLES

Aside from fruit and veggie scraps and yard trimmings, you will come across a motley assortment of items that you can toss into a compost bin. As you become more and more experienced/obsessed with composting, you'll probably find more to add to this list:

High Carbon

- Cotton swabs (cotton/cardboard swabs only—no plastic!)
- Tissues
- Dryer lint
- Wood ash
- Paper towels
- Matches (extinguished and cooled, of course)
- Nut shells
- Feathers from old pillows
- Vacuum cleaner dust

High Nitrogen

- Soymilk and almond milk
- Tofu
- Old wine and beer
- Urine

Neither High Nitrogen nor High Carbon

- Eggshells
- Pet hair
- Human hair
- Nail clippings
- Old potting soil

▲ Eggshells add important minerals to finished compost, but they tend to take a very long time to break down.

◄ Cotton swabs with no plastic will completely decompose in your compost pile.

Leaf bins provide the perfect place for an occasional addition of urine.

Our local soil and water conservation district conducted a study that sampled finished compost from seven different residential compost piles. One sample stood out as having a much higher level of available nitrogen than the others (327 ppm versus the average of 110 ppm). When they asked the homeowner how he created such fantastically balanced compost, he sheepishly admitted to regularly peeing on the leaf pile.

Yes, urine (both pet and human) makes a fantastic addition to a compost pile. High in nitrogen, urine acts as an accelerator to help carbon-rich dry leaves decompose faster. How you get the urine to the compost pile, well, that's up to you.

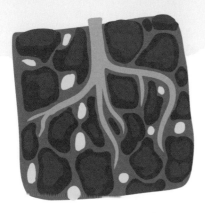

◀ Maintaining the perfect amount of moisture in your compost pile will coat each particle with water and allow air to move through the materials.

THE YIN AND YANG OF OXYGEN AND WATER

Our composting microorganisms need air to breathe and water to survive. Too much of one cancels out the other, however, so a successful composter maintains a pile moist enough to provide our microbe friends enough water to survive but not so much that the pile has no oxygen. If the pile is about as wet as a wrung-out sponge, a film of water will coat each particle in the bin but have pockets of air surrounding the particle. This thin film of water on the surface of particles is where most of the microbe activity happens.

If you pick up (wearing gloves) a handful of compost matter and squeeze, that material should not release more than a few drops of water. If the compost crackles in your hands into a dry crispiness, it needs water. If you can squeeze a shower out of the compost, then the pile has too much water.

The simple act of adding food scraps likely supplies your compost with all necessary water most of the year. If you live in a very hot climate or during the peak heat of summer, adding water to your pile will help keep your microorganisms alive. To avoid the chlorinated water

▲ Cutting material into smaller pieces will help your microorganism friends decompose the scraps faster.

◀ Leave water in a bucket for a few hours so the chlorine evaporates before adding the water to your compost.

coming from most hoses, fill a bucket with water and allow the chlorine a few hours to evaporate before watering your pile. You can also use water from your rain barrel if you have one.

If your pile is too wet, add dry leaves or shredded paper to help soak up the water. Leaving the lid off (if you have one) will also help the excess moisture escape as long as Mother Nature does not rain on your parade.

PARTICLE SIZE

Particle size is another factor affecting the air flow through your pile. Imagine the difference in the size of sawdust and wood chips: Wood chips will have vastly more air space between the particles than the sawdust. The sawdust offers easier eating (more available carbon) to our microbe friends. As they decompose the sawdust particles, microorganisms will quickly consume the air in between the tiny particles, effectively ending their feast prematurely. Balancing the need for air and your microbe friends' desire for fast food will give you the fastest composting results.

KEEPING MATERIAL SMALL

Our microinvertebrate friends will eat any organic thing you throw in the compost bin, but if you want them to eat faster, make the pieces smaller. Chopping up the material increases the surface area for the bacteria and fungi. Cutting up large (hello, pumpkins) or dense (look out, broccoli stalks) material will help your microorganisms create finished compost in much less time.

Add dry materials such as leaves and straw and aerate your compost regularly to avoid anaerobic bacteria taking over.

A composter with multiple units should be aerated using a pitchfork. Simply "fork" the material from one unit to the next.

AEROBIC VERSUS ANAEROBIC

Not all decomposition is equal, and what happens in your compost pile will either fall into the anaerobic or the aerobic category. If we water our compost too much or do not provide enough air, we can create an environment where only the anaerobic bacteria want to live. For most types of backyard composting, the anaerobic bacteria are the bad guys. (No offense to the little buggers; they just do what comes naturally.)

Anaerobic bacteria break down material s-l-o-w-l-y and create smelly gases that will make even the stoutest of composters lose their lunch. Another word for anaerobic decomposition is putrefaction. Swamps owe their distinctive odors to anaerobic bacteria, and aside from a few specialized forms of composting, we do not want to replicate this slow, slimy, smelly decomposition in our backyards.

As if you needed more reason to dislike anaerobic decomposition in backyard composting, this type of decomposition releases mostly methane gas instead of the CO_2 released during aerobic decomposition. Methane absorbs more energy in our atmosphere than does carbon dioxide, resulting in a global warming potential twenty-five times higher than carbon dioxide.

Aerobic, or air-loving, bacteria are the good guys. They decompose material quickly and with little to no odor. We want to do everything we can to invite them in and have them stay a while.

MAINTAINING AIR POCKETS IN YOUR COMPOST

We've already discussed our friends in depth—the aerobic, air-loving microorganisms that perform the bulk of the work in turning our "garbage" into luscious, wonderful compost. One of the essential needs of our air-loving friends is, of course, air. The more food scraps and leaves you add to the pile, the more the weight compacts the layers, pushing out the air pockets our friends need to do their job. To keep our aerobic microorganisms happy, we must add air back in. Adding air gives the microorganisms room to multiply and speeds up decomposition. How do we get air into a giant pile of stuff?

If you have a tumbler, aeration is simple: a quick spin of the bin gives you all the air you need. If you have a two- or three-unit setup designed for moving piles from one unit to the next, then your pitchfork and back muscles will be adding air on a regular basis. Having a multiple-unit composter or a pile gives you the advantage of "easy" pile turning using a

above **Tumbler-style composters are the easiest to turn and add air to your compost.** *right* **This DIY auger will aerate the pile to speed up composting but will not substantially mix or turn the materials in the pile for an even decomposition.**

pitchfork. The act of moving compost from one side to the next (or moving it from one spot to the next with an open pile) gives the compost a nice boost of oxygen.

Aerating the Pile

For the traditional black plastic bin with an open bottom, using a specialized aerating tool will help you create air pockets in just a few minutes of stabbing. Aerating tools generally have a sharp end and little metal or plastic flaps that protrude out as you pull the tool up. A pointy stick would also help add some air into the pile; you just have to do a little more stabbing than with the specialized tools. Depending on how your day went, you may find stabbing something with a pointy stick quite therapeutic.

After you turn the pile, you will notice the compost heating up and decreasing in size over the next few days or weeks. Take this as a good sign that your pile is doing what it is supposed to do.

You can choose the eager or the lazy route when it comes to aeration. Once a week will earn you an A and finished compost in a few short months. Once-a-month aeration also works well, and you will have finished compost in nine months to a year. I know lazy composters who never turn their piles and still harvest beautiful compost. You do risk the pile going anaerobic by not turning it, but everyone's backyard, neighbors, and lifestyles are different.

Turning Versus Aerating

Many composters, myself included, are guilty of using the terms *aerating* and *turning* interchangeably. Some methods of aerating a pile also turn the materials, such as with a compost tumbler or with a multi-unit bin where you physically move the pile with a pitchfork. Most aeration techniques, including augers, simply supply air to the microorganisms in the pile.

Turning a compost pile moves the material on the outside of the pile into the hot center to more thoroughly decompose. Turning also ensures that those materials will reach a high temperature, killing weed seeds and pathogens. If you want faster decomposition, physically stir your materials at least once during your composting process. This may require removing the plastic compost bin off your pile and scooping everything back into the bin. Even without turning, your materials will eventually decompose, perhaps just not as quickly or evenly as possible.

BASIC COMPOSTING TOOLS (The Starter Kit)

Compost Bin While not essential (as you will see in chapter 4), a compost bin acts as a vessel to keep material contained and protected. Compost bins come in many shapes and sizes, and chapter 3 will help you select one suitable for your yard and lifestyle.

Aerator An aerator lets you easily add air to the pile with less work than a pitchfork. One end of the aerator generally has a handle, and the other end connects to an auger-type device that fluffs up the compacted parts of the pile, leaving air pockets in its wake.

Pitchfork or Spading Fork Nothing moves manure and wet compost better than a pitchfork. The tines of the fork slice through the compost while the wetness of the materials hold the clump you scooped up together on the pitchfork. Unless the compost is very dry, you will exert less effort using a pitchfork than a spade or a shovel.

The term *pitchfork* traditionally describes pitchforks with more delicate tines designed to scoop lightweight material like straw or hay, such as the one featured in the iconic *American Gothic* painting. These slender tines could bend under the heavier weight of compost.

What I use—and what most gardeners call a pitchfork—is technically a spading fork. These very tough tools generally have four or five strong tines and a robust wooden handle. They take a beating with no complaint. When I refer to a pitchfork in this book, a spading fork is the tool I have in mind.

Wheelbarrow A wheelbarrow comes in handy for many garden tasks and becomes especially helpful when you harvest your compost. Slightly wet, heavy, and plentiful finished compost simply must be proudly paraded around your yard in a wheelbarrow. Sometimes I admire my wheelbarrow of finished compost just for fun before spreading it around my garden.

Kitchen Collector A designated vessel to collect scraps in your kitchen will make you much more likely to compost your food scraps. These come in fancy stainless-steel or bamboo models, or they can be as simple as a plastic bucket. Kitchen collectors remind everyone else in your house to place that banana peel in the compost pail instead of the trash.

Personal preference will dictate your degree of fanciness, but you could even reuse an old coffee can or an old butter tub. Fruit flies travel into your home on produce from the grocery store, so having a lid will help deter those pesky critters from living in your scraps. A handle is also nice but not essential.

Since my kids consume copious amounts of fruit, I need an even larger container and use a small can with a foot pedal next to my regular garbage can. The small trash can used to collect diapers when I had babies, but we repurposed it as a scrap collector. The foot pedal helps when you approach the container with hands full of scraps.

Shovel or Spade A good sharp shovel (sometimes called a spade) could be your best friend in the garden and when you compost. I drag both my pitchfork and shovel with me when I harvest my compost and use my shovel to distribute the compost around my garden, usually as mulch. If you plan on using the integrated composting techniques in chapter 4, your shovel will be by your side.

clockwise, left to right **An aerating tool creates air pockets in your pile, speeding up decomposition. A pitchfork and a wheelbarrow are two incredibly useful tools for composters. This stainless-steel kitchen scrap collector features a carbon filter and tight-fitting lid that will keep in odors and keep out flies. Screening compost removes large materials and allows the beautiful finished compost to fall underneath. A small repurposed trash can with a foot pedal collects food scraps in my kitchen.**

Screener Screening pulls out the peach pits, unfinished clumps of unidentifiable muck, sticks, and sometimes even produce stickers. All the unfinished stuff can go back into your compost bin as treasure for another day. You can read more about the joys of screening compost in chapter 7.

Hand Cultivator or Garden Fork Reaching into your compost with bare hands is usually a risky proposition. Those seemingly benign leaves could be hiding a gooey, rotten melon filled with maggots. If you would rather not play Russian roulette with your compost pile, invest in a small hand cultivator or garden fork. This handheld tool acts like an extension of your hand, allowing you to pull back the top layer of the pile and neatly tuck the food scraps in for their nap. I keep one next to my compost bin and use it every day when adding scraps to the pile.

COMPOST HAPPENS

Obviously, decomposition happens in nature and is an essential part of the nutrient cycle to transform the finite matter on this planet from death to life and back again. As composters, we attempt, usually successfully, to somewhat control this process in our backyards by creating the best habitat for our favorite decomposers and combining old leaves and leftover food scraps in the hopes of producing something wonderful.

I find that remembering the "little people" who do the actual work in the compost pile (e.g., the bacteria, fungi, earthworms, etc.) helps me maintain a successful composting system. Like guests at a party, I want them to be happy and have everything they need. When I dig into my compost, I can imagine billions upon billions of bacteria quietly munching away, and I want to do what I can to support their efforts. In perspective, our work as composters pales compared to what all our micro and macro friends contribute. Thanks, little buddies—we appreciate that you make our compost party possible!

This unscreened compost will make a valuable soil amendment and still has an earthworm munching away.

KITCHEN COLLECTOR LINER

||||||||||||||||||||||||||||||||||||||||

This simple liner keeps your food scraps contained in a nice package, soaks up excess liquids, and acts as a source of carbon when you toss the package in the compost bin. You will never again have to bang the kitchen pail on the side of your compost bin while attempting to dislodge potato peels and tea leaves stuck to the bottom.

MATERIALS NEEDED:

▶ Black-and-white newspaper

▶ Scissors (or excellent tearing skills)

TIME NEEDED: 10 minutes

LET'S DO IT

STEP 1. Stack three or four pieces of newspaper together.

STEP 2. Fold one corner down to the opposite edge to create a triangle.

STEP 3. Cut the excess newspaper off the triangle. (If you were to unfold the triangle, it would make a square.)

STEP 4. Fold one corner (**A**) bordering the original fold down to the center of the other side.

STEP 5. Fold the other corner (**B**) bordered by the original fold over to the center of the opposite side.

STEP 6. Now find the last point of your triangle, the only corner (**C**) with free paper on either side. Fold several layers of paper down over the other paper to create an opening. Fold the rest of the layers down on the other side.

STEP 7. Open up the area you just folded back and you have a paper liner. Alternatively, you can also use this to create a very fashionable hat.

DIY liner instructions come from Green Bin Ottawa.

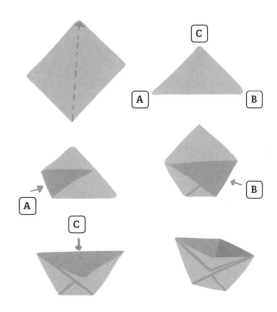

The newspaper liner is only a little more complicated than a paper airplane once you get the hang of it.

A newspaper liner keeps your kitchen collector clean and adds brown material to the compost with your food scraps.

Troubleshooting Problems

PROBLEM	CAUSE	SOLUTION
Pile smells garbagy.	Food scraps are exposed or too close to surface.	Bury your food scraps with leaves every time you add food scraps.
Pile has a strong ammonia smell.	Pile has too much nitrogen (green).	Add more carbon (brown) material, such as dry brown leaves, shredded newspaper, or cardboard.
Pile smells like a swamp or rotten eggs.	Pile has too much moisture/water.	Leave the lid off your bin and incorporate dry material until it is as wet as a wrung-out sponge.
Pile is not decomposing.	Pile is too dry, too small, or needs more nitrogen.	Make sure your pile is as wet as a wrung-out sponge, add more material until your pile is 3 × 3 × 3 feet (90 × 90 × 90 cm), and add high-nitrogen material such as food scraps.
Pile has lots of sticks or matted leaves.	Material is too large to decompose.	Shred or break apart the material before you place it in the compost pile.
Ants, bees, or some other annoying pests are living in my bin.	Pile is not hot enough to discourage unwanted guests.	Turn the pile and add some high-nitrogen material, such as food scraps or grass clippings.
Plants are growing in my bin.	You either have finished compost that needs harvesting, or your pile is not hot enough.	Harvest the finished compost or aerate the pile to encourage it to heat up.

A QUICK WAY TO GET RID OF FRUIT FLIES

Fruit flies are the tiny but pesky flying insects that seem to appear out of nowhere to swarm your kitchen collector and compost bin, especially during the summer. These little buggers actually ride into your home on your produce as larvae or eggs (just another reason to wash that apple before you eat it). Aside from pulling out a miniature fly swatter, you can take a few easy steps to discourage or reduce their nuisance.

If a swarm of fruit flies seems to attack you when you lift the lid of your compost bin, you need to bury your food scraps. These small insects will not burrow down into a pile to lay their eggs on your food scraps. If you cover the scraps with leaves, the flies will venture elsewhere.

Occasionally, these flies appear in your kitchen. (Don't worry, they bother non-composters, too.) You can take preventive action here.

Ideas for discouraging fruit flies in your kitchen:

- ▸ Take out your kitchen scraps daily or several times a day when flies are in your kitchen.
- ▸ Cover food scraps added to your kitchen collector with sawdust.
- ▸ Use a kitchen collector with a tight-fitting lid.
- ▸ Create a fruit-fly trap.

You can create a simple fruit-fly trap with a small plastic container with a clear lid. Poke several holes in the clear lid. Place aa banana peel and some apple cider vinegar in the container, replace the lid, and set the container in an area where the flies congregate. The sweet smells from the apple cider vinegar and banana peel will draw the flies in through the holes, but they cannot escape. If the plight of the poor imprisoned flies pulls at your heartstrings, you can release them into the wild (your backyard)—just stay away from your compost bin.

Banana peel and apple cider vinegar attract fruit flies through small holes in the top of your trap. Once in, flies cannot find a way back out.

Low-Maintenance Outdoor Composting

‖‖‖‖‖‖‖‖‖‖‖‖‖‖‖‖‖‖‖‖‖‖‖‖‖‖‖‖‖

COMPOST IN A BACKYARD BIN

Perhaps the easiest and most common type of home composting is designating a small space in your backyard for an enclosed composting vessel. One project in this chapter may appeal to you more than the others, depending on the space you have, the materials you need to compost, how quickly you want finished compost, and how attractive a compost bin you desire.

Manufactured compost bins usually work well, so if you are not inclined to make your own bin and have a little extra cash, don't feel guilty about forgoing the DIY projects to buy a bin. You can even find used compost bins on social media and online yard sale–like platforms, sometimes even for free.

CHOOSE THE RIGHT COMPOSTER FOR YOU

This chapter goes over four basic DIY backyard compost bins. If you do not have a backyard space, skip to chapter 5. To integrate composting into your garden rather than using a bin, skip to chapter 4. Or you can read this chapter anyway and appreciate all of the snazzy projects.

The Reused Pickle Barrel Composter (page 43) creates a low-cost plastic bin that functions like the composters you buy in the store at a fraction of the cost. This works perfectly for someone with only a few square feet of space who wants to compost kitchen scraps and a small quantity of leaves or other yard debris.

clockwise from top left **Premade compost bins work well to compost the average-size family's food scraps and a limited amount of your leaves. The Compact Salvaged Pallet Bin comes together in 2 hours and can compost all of your kitchen scraps and yard trimmings, maybe even with contributions from your neighbors. The Simple Leftover Fence Bin requires minimal tools and less than a half hour of work.**

The Compact Salvaged Pallet Bin (page 46) steps in as the pickle barrel's larger cousin. It requires a little more space but should be able to compost most of your leaves and yard trimmings as well as kitchen scraps.

Want something a little more mobile? The Repurposed Trash Can Tumbler (page 52) would make an excellent bin that can easily move around the yard while you weed but also tuck away in a corner out of sight. This tumbler is small and best used with batch composting. (I'll explain more later.)

Finally, the Simple Leftover Fence Bin (page 54) provides a perfect place to compost leaves and weeds pulled from your yard. Pair this with the Reused Pickle Barrel Composter for a perfect composting duo.

LOCATION, LOCATION, LOCATION: FINDING JUST THE RIGHT SPOT

When scouting your backyard for a composting location, look for these qualities:

▶ Protection from too much sun or wind
▶ Good drainage
▶ Easy access from your home

A sunny spot will help heat up your pile, but intense sunlight could also cause your pile to dry out. I find that shady or partially sunny spots require less maintenance—especially watering—in the long run. A pile with the right balance of brown and green will heat up even in the shadiest of locations. Like too much sun, too much wind can also dry out your pile, so consider the exposure of an area to strong winds before setting up your compost.

While you may want your pile to stay moist, too much water can cause catastrophe. Choose a location that drains well and does not hold water when it rains. Standing water will create a mucky, smelly mess in your compost. A good way to scope out an area's drainage is to watch what happens during and after a rainfall. If a spot forms a small pond when it rains, avoid setting up a compost pile in that spot, or your backyard may smell like a swamp.

Imagine it is late at night and you are cleaning up your kitchen in your slippers. You glance at your overflowing food scrap bucket and realize you still need to take your kitchen scraps to the compost bin. Is your location close enough to the house to allow a quick trot from your door to the bin? What about in the winter? Will you still be able to make the trek then? Locating the pile conveniently close to the house increases your chances of following through on adding those precious food scraps to your pile even when you are busy or in less-than-ideal weather. If your bin lives too far away from your back door, you may decide not to make the trip and pitch those valuable food scraps in the trash.

Avoid Potential Problem Areas

NEAR TREES (ESPECIALLY SMALL OR MEDIUM TREES): When I purchased my first home, I placed my backyard compost bin in a spot that seemed perfectly cozy along the property line under a medium-size tree that stood in my neighbor's yard. During the first harvest, I learned why placing a compost bin directly under a tree is a bad idea. I had created beautiful compost, but the neighboring tree had grown its roots up into the pile. I spent hours battling and hacking

If you place your compost bin too close to a small tree or shrub, you may have to battle for access to your bin.

(sorry, tree) at roots to pull any usable compost from my bin. After that disaster, I moved my bin to the other side of the yard, out of the reach of any overeager trees. Very large trees with deep roots do not seem to have the same inclination to steal your compost.

AGAINST A WOOD FENCE: Wood fences may seem like a natural fit to act as one side of your compost bin, but compost bins decompose organic matter—and your wood fence is organic matter even if it is treated or painted. Eventually, that fence will become part of the compost pile and decompose. My guess is that your neighbor would be none-too-happy if your compost peeked through the fence to say hello. Leave at least a foot (30 cm) of space between your bin and a wood fence.

DIRECTLY NEXT TO YOUR HOME: Composting encourages bugs of all sorts. While we are happy to create that space for the crawling critters in the compost bin, we do not want to invite them inside our homes. Place your compost a few feet (1 m) away from your home to discourage any unwanted houseguests.

REUSED PICKLE BARREL COMPOSTER

|||||||||||||||||||||||||||||||||||||||||

The idea of upcycling a pickle barrel into a composter came from my husband, who used an old pickle barrel as a rain barrel for our home. How many pickles could our family possibly eat, you ask? Why do we have so many excess pickle barrels lying about? Well, although we love the sour, salty, crunchy treat, I purchased these used barrels from a local pickle manufacturer for $10 apiece. On a tip from a friend, I just called them up and asked if they would sell me a few used barrels. Should you not be so lucky to have a friendly neighborhood pickle factory, consider what other food manufacturers in your area that may have similar barrels.

Genius husbands and pickle factories aside, this fantastic project results in a compost bin resembling something you might buy online for $100 plus shipping. The tools involved are minimal and I included a few easy ideas to spruce up the black plastic should you want to feature the bin in your garden.

MATERIALS NEEDED:

- Pickle barrel or similar industrial barrel used for food
- Gloves
- Drill with ⅜-inch bit
- Chisel
- Jigsaw
- Measuring tape
- Wire fencing
- Tin snips
- Staple gun and staples
- Pliers
- Hammer
- Shovel

SPACE NEEDED: 2.5 × 2.5 feet (75 × 75 cm)

TIME NEEDED: 2 hours

LET'S DO IT

STEP 1. First, you need to cut off the bottom of the barrel just before it tapers. Wearing gloves, set the barrel on its side and start the cut using a drill or chisel. Once the hole is big enough, use a jigsaw to saw off the bottom. You will eventually bury this edge under the ground, so don't fret if it is not perfect.

Easy and cheap to make, this Reused Pickle Barrel Composter will compost food scraps and leaves for the average-size family.

After starting the cut with a chisel, use a jigsaw to cut off the bottom of the barrel just before it starts to taper.

Drill airholes every 2 inches (5 cm) into the sides of the barrel. Asking someone to keep the barrel from rolling away will make this job easier.

STEP 1. Next, we will make vent holes for the side of the bin. Use a measuring tape (and a level if you strive for perfection) and mark holes every 2 inches (5 cm) up the sides. We made four rows of ten holes. Drilling holes into the plastic will create little curlicue plastic shavings, so this is best done over a driveway or other easily sweepable surface.

STEP 2. Next, we will improve the lid. If you can easily screw on and off your lid, I would recommend skipping this step and maybe just drilling a few air holes in the top. However, the pickle barrel I purchased had a two-part lid: a very tight-fitting inner lid that would be a struggle to remove every day and a threaded outer lid that held it in place. We removed that inner lid and created a "new" lid using the threaded outer lid.

Trace a circle of wire mesh 1 inch (2.5 cm) or so larger than your opening in the outer lid. Use tin snips to snip the wire into a circle. Press the wire mesh circle into the top of the threaded outer lid. Staple the wire into place from the top down through to the inside every 2 inches (5 cm). Be generous with the staples so you don't snag yourself later. You will now have the pointy ends of the staples pointing down on the underside of your lid. Flip the lid upside down and use the pliers to bend the ends down and the hammer to flatten.

STEP 3. Push the bin into the ground in the spot you want it to live to mark the spot. Remove the bin and use a shovel to dig around the circle 2 to 3 inches (5 to 7.5 cm) into the ground to stabilize it. Place the bin in its new home and pile soil around the outside.

Staple the wire mesh through the top of lid to secure.

Burying the Pickle Barrel Composter a few inches into the ground will give it more stability.

Burying the bin a few inches will provide it with stability and make knocking the bin over more difficult for curious creatures. Start the bin with a foot (30 cm) of leaves (shredded if you can) and keep adding material as needed. This bin will not have much natural airflow, so aerate with an aeration tool or stick every once in a while. Because it holds in moisture and allows rainwater through the top, it likely will not need to be watered in most climates.

You can use the bin as is, or you can get creative and decorate the outside to match your style. I found a "terra-cotta" colored spray paint for plastic at my local hardware store, so I gave that a go for this project. The composter took only 15 minutes to paint and the paint stuck surprisingly well. You could paint flowers, leaves, stripes, polka dots, zig zags, gnomes, wombats, whatever your heart desires. After a few years, I imagine this paint will fade and need a refresh.

To harvest compost from this bin, simply lift the bin off the pile to reveal the material inside. Chapter 7 will go into more detail on harvesting and using your finished compost.

 BRIGHT IDEA: Use the bottom of the barrel as a flower pot, container for organizing, or, if you are six like my daughter, a swimming pool for your dolls.

COMPACT SALVAGED PALLET BIN

||||||||||||||||||||||||||||||||||||||||||||

Raise your hand if you want to make composting as easy as possible. If you have a 4-foot × 4-foot (1.2- × 1.2-m) area in your backyard and a few hours, you can be the proud owner of this cool pallet compost bin. It seems people use shipping pallets to make everything these days, from stylish lawn furniture to trendy feature walls behind a couch. We will keep this project simple by using the pallets for the most part intact, but feel free to expand on these instructions and build something even fancier.

Using shipping pallets to create a compost bin has many benefits. They are easy to find, and you can usually score pallets for free. They are the perfect size, the wood is already cut, and the spaces between the slats provide great airflow, which means finished compost sooner.

But where can I find shipping pallets, you ask? First, ask the facilities person at your workplace. No luck there? Small businesses receive pallets with shipments and may just toss them in the dumpster, so ask around. I saw a stack of pallets outside my local reuse center and asked if I could have a few. Post the question on social media and you will be surprised how many people have old pallets they would love to offload.

Look for pallets that have been heat treated rather than chemically treated to preserve the wood. Heat-treated pallets usually have an "HT" stamped on them somewhere. Used pallets are ideal, because we are giving them a second life, but look for pallets with a lighter color. Shipping pallets work hard in their first life, but the lighter color pallets generally have seen less weathering and harsh treatment and are not as close to rotting as their darker more brittle brothers.

Try to choose pallets measuring close to the same size so they easily fit together. At least try to have the pallets all the same height and have "pairs" of pallets that match the length of the opposite side. You want to make as close to a square or rectangle as possible, not a wobbly polygon.

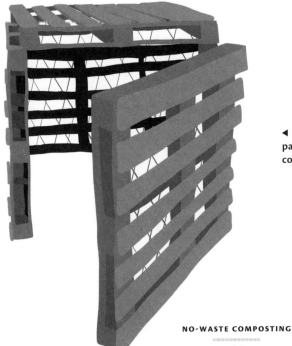

◀ An easy-to-open front panel simplifies harvesting compost from this pallet bin.

MATERIALS NEEDED:

- ▶ Gloves
- ▶ 4 shipping pallets
- ▶ Screws
- ▶ Drill
- ▶ Chicken wire or hardware cloth
- ▶ Staple gun and staples
- ▶ Tin snips
- ▶ 4 eye-hooks or latches
- ▶ OPTIONAL: outdoor stain, metal hinges, and fifth pallet for lid

SPACE NEEDED: 4 × 4 feet (1.2 × 1.2 m)
TIME NEEDED: 3 hours

Used pallets make a low-cost, timesaving material with which to build a bin.

LET'S DO IT

STEP 1. Choose a flat surface with enough room to access the front of the compost bin. Wearing gloves, set up the four pallets to make sure they fit together. The side with the slats closer together should be on the outside. If possible, have the slats run horizontally, as this seems to hold the materials in the bin better. If the pallets sit together better vertically though, this will work just fine.

STEP 2. Use the screws to attach the left and back pallets together at the top and bottom at a right angle. Then do the same to attach the right pallet to the back pallet. Drill pilot holes by predrilling with a bit smaller in diameter than your screw to reduce the chance of your wood splitting.

STEP 3. Line the inside of the three sides with chicken wire, hardware cloth, or other sturdy mesh-like material. This is easiest with a staple gun. Use tin snips to make the mesh the right size. Bring the mesh about 1 inch (2.5 cm) from the top of the bin to protect you from annoying stray wires scraping your skin.

Look for pallets with an "HT" stamp, meaning they have been heat treated to preserve the wood rather than treated with chemicals.

Securing the pallets together with screws may require drilling at an angle.

Use a staple gun to attach wire mesh to the inside of the three sides. This mesh will hold in your compostables more securely than the pallets alone and discourage unwanted guests to your bin.

Attach the front panel at all four corners with eye-hooks so you can easily remove at harvest time.

STEP 1. Now use the fourth pallet to create the front. Cut a piece of chicken wire or other metal mesh to fit the front pallet and staple it to the inside. Again, this should stretch to about 1 inch (2.5 cm) from the top of the pallet.

STEP 2. Attach the front pallet with eye-hooks or latches at the four corners. This will allow you easy access to the bin for harvesting. You will only open this once or twice per year, so, alternatively, you could just screw it on and unscrew it when it is time to harvest.

Ta-da! Now you have a fresh pallet bin, ready to use. If you are worried about critters hanging out in your compost, you could build a lid to help keep them out. Remember, the lid needs to be large enough to connect the four pallets yet light enough to lift. You also want rainwater to easily filter through.

OPTIONAL LID: To create a lid, line the inside of the pallet with chicken wire or mesh as you did the other pallets. Attach the lid with hinges on one side or the back. I find a side opening lid easier to manage when bringing food scraps to the compost.

If you have space, you could create a two-unit bin so one bin "cooks" while you add to the other. In the harvesting chapter, I explain how to harvest compost if you have only one bin. Not digging the raw wood look of the pallets? Stain the outside for a more polished look. Do not stain the inside of the bin to avoid putting unnecessary chemicals into your compost. Pallets also act as an excellent trellis, so you could plant some vining plants around the sides of the bin (not the front) that will camouflage the compost into the garden.

Attaching a pallet as a lid will keep animals out of your new bin.

This Compact Salvaged Pallet Bin has plenty of space for all of your yard trimmings and food scraps.

OFF TO A SUCCESSFUL START

Once you have a bin and a location, you will be eager to get the party, otherwise known as the compost pile, started. Beginning with a few feet (60 to 90 cm) of shredded brown leaves will give your pile a nice base layer from which to grow. Shredded leaves will break down much faster, but if time is not an issue for you, adding whole leaves works too.

If you collect kitchen scraps, dump the scraps on top of the leaves and then cover them with more leaves. You should not be able to see any scraps peeking out. Add weeds you pull from the yard or small trimmings from plants as you have them. Sprinkle on a shovelful of healthy garden soil (not the sterile stuff you buy in a bag) on top of the pile to jump-start the decomposing organisms. Keep bringing out your food scraps and burying them with leaves, and soon micro- and macroorganisms will have populated the pile, rip-roaring your compost into action.

Starting your compost bin off with a few feet of leaves will give the pile a good base layer.

MAKE YOUR OWN COMPOST BIN

I know that some people reading this would much rather build their own composter from materials found at a building materials reuse store or hardware store rather than follow step-by-step instructions. I've pulled together a few things to remember as you consider creating and constructing your bin.

You probably want your compost bin to have these traits:

- Approximately 3 × 3 × 3 feet (90 × 90 × 90 cm) in size
- Open to soil underneath
- Critter-proof
- Easy access to add scraps
- Good airflow or ability to aerate
- Allows rain through the top or enclosed to hold in moisture
- Attractive (subject to personal taste)

There are also some things you don't want for your compost bin. As you look around a building material reuse store, avoid these materials:

- Anything that will decompose quickly (unless you are okay with building again really soon).

- Items that might contaminate your compost, such as something painted with lead paint. My advice is to avoid anything painted.
- Breakable material, such as old glass double-hung windows (but glass blocks might work).

When my husband and I were walking around our local building reuse center, we talked about what pieces would make good compost bins. Items such as shutters (especially aluminum), plastic vinyl siding, railroad ties, leftover pavers, and doors seemed like good candidates. We discussed how the hardware could be attached if needed, how a bin could be harvested, and whether it could easily be moved around a yard or stay in one place. You may also want to consider logistics of storing your leaves in your bin design. If you can't find everything you need at the reuse store you may need to go to the hardware store, to supplement your materials, especially for hardware or tools.

left **Shopping at a building materials reuse center is a cost-saving way to start a project.** *right* **These leftover pavers could build a simple composting bay that is open on one side for easy turning.**

TUMBLER-STYLE COMPOSTERS

The Grateful Dead of composters, tumblers have a loyal and dedicated following. These bins are up off the ground in some barrel-type contraption that either spins or rolls to add air to the compost. Tumblers will make finished compost fast if you know how to maintain them.

Composting in a tumbler is more hands-on than other methods. They have the advantage of being easy to turn, which means you will add air more often than with a traditional compost bin. Adding that air helps activate the good bacteria and heat up the compost material quickly. Some composters claim to harvest finished compost in just a few weeks with their tumbler.

The biggest mistake composters make when using tumblers is adding too many food scraps and not enough brown material. Food scraps will turn into a sloshy, stinky mess without the balance of the dry brown material.

You also need to carefully monitor the moisture level with tumblers. Composters on the ground have the advantage of easily draining into the soil if too much moisture builds up. Even tumblers with drain holes can accumulate too much water (again—sloshy, stinky mess). If you squeeze your compost (gloves on, remember) and you can squeeze out a significant amount of water, it is too wet and needs shredded paper or leaves immediately.

Because tumblers have limited contact with the soil, they do not benefit from migrating microorganisms as a traditional bin does. Add a few shovelfuls of good living soil from your yard or purchase beneficial microorganisms. After your first batch, keep a little of the old compost behind to inoculate the new material.

Tumblers also require that you stop adding materials to the bin about 3 weeks before you plan to harvest. Tumblers work best using batch composting. When you batch compost, you add a lot of material all at once rather than a little at a time. You wouldn't pull cookies out of the oven halfway through baking to add more flour, so don't add more food scraps while your tumbler finishes the compost decomposition. Freeze the food scraps in the meantime or use the pit or trench techniques in chapter 4 until you are ready to start a new batch.

BRIGHT IDEA

Batch composting, or adding a larger volume of material at one time, speeds up decomposition because the larger volume heats up faster. Batch composting works well with tumblers and hot composting (see "Hot Composting" in chapter 4), but you can use the concept with any method. Coming up with a larger volume of material may require you to strategically freeze your food scraps for a few weeks and collect coffee grounds from your neighborhood coffee shop.

Adding a larger volume of material at one time will create a batch of compost that will quickly decompose in the tumbler.

REPURPOSED TRASH CAN TUMBLER

If you want to start using a tumbler-style composter but find your eyebrows raising when you see their prices, this next DIY project is for you. In about a half hour and making use of materials you likely already have, you can create a rolling tumbler that makes up for its trashy looks by working beautifully. "Trashy" meaning it's made out of an old trash can, so you may want to tuck it out of sight if it doesn't fit your garden aesthetic.

Don't have a spare trash can with a lid? Consider reaching out to your neighbors and friends through social media. You will be surprised how many people have extra trash cans lying around that they can't bring themselves to "trash."

MATERIALS NEEDED:

- 1 plastic trash can with lid, about 15-gallon (57-L) size
- Soap and water (if using used trash can)
- Gloves
- Drill and ⅜-inch bit (or similar)
- 2 bungee cords

SPACE NEEDED: 2 × 2 feet (60 × 60 cm)
TIME NEEDED: ½ hour

LET'S DO IT

STEP 1. Clean out the can with soap and water if it was used to hold garbage. No reason to start with a smelly can.

STEP 2. Wearing gloves, drill holes in the sides of the can every 2 inches (5 cm). We drilled twelve holes on two opposite sides.

STEP 3. Drill holes in the bottom at the lowest point so any liquid can drain and will not collect in the bottom when the composter is upright.

STEP 4. Start by filling the can with shredded leaves or another brown material. If you have enough food scraps and yard trimmings to fill it three-fourths full, then you have enough for a batch compost. Alternatively, fill it with what you have right now and add more later.

Drill holes every 2 inches (5 cm) to allow for better airflow.

Drill holes in the bottom so liquid can easily drain.

Fill your tumbler with two to three parts brown material for every one part green material.

To turn your new trash can tumbler, tilt it on the side and roll.

STEP 5. Secure the lid with the bungees by looping the bungees over the lid and clasping to the handle on the other side. If your can does not have a handle, you can use the drill to create a hole to secure the bungees.

STEP 6. To turn the bin, simply lay the can on its side and roll. Try to do this at least once per week.

If you fill the bin three-fourths full and roll it around every few days, you should have finished compost in 6 weeks to 2 months. If you are adding slowly, try to keep a balance of two parts brown to one part green. Keep turning every week and adding material until it is pretty full (no more than three-fourths). After you stop adding material, keep turning weekly and you will have finished compost a few months later.

SIMPLE LEFTOVER FENCE BIN

||||||||||||||||||||||||||||||||||||

Fence bins take the award for the easiest bin to build. One step up from just piling material on the ground, they keep leaves and yard trimmings in a nice contained area while not looking obtrusive next to landscaping. Wire bins and their counterparts make fantastic vessels for holding the large amount of leaves dumped each year on those of us living with deciduous trees. By containing the leaves and yard trimmings in a certain area, you speed up decomposition and help maintain a tidier yard.

You can use almost any wire fencing or even plastic fencing to build these bins yourself. You can also choose any type of fastener to hold the bin in place. Metal wire, carabiners, or even twist ties will do the trick in a pinch.

A word of caution: fence bins do not make super places to compost food scraps. Squirrels, raccoons, mice, and deer can usually munch on your leftovers. If you don't want to feed the local wildlife, stick with adding leaves and yard trimmings to this type of bin. If you do add food scraps, bury them in a few feet of leaves to make the bin less tempting to critters foraging for food.

Building a leaf bin from leftover fencing is easy peasy. It will probably take you more time to gather the supplies than to actually construct the bin. Depending on the annual bounty of leaves you expect in your yard, you may want to build multiple structures or a larger bin. A 3-foot (90-cm)-tall leaf bin with a 3-foot (90-cm) diameter will hold the same amount of leaves as five paper leaf bags. A 3-foot (90-cm)-tall leaf bin with a 4-foot (1.2-m) diameter will hold the same amount of leaves as nine paper leaf bags.

Leaves will settle quickly in a leaf bin, usually shrinking to half their original volume in just a month or two. With any luck, a full leaf bin will make room for more leaves before the next time you have to rake.

These instructions will build a 3-foot (90-cm)-diameter bin. For a 4-foot (1.2-m)-diameter bin, you'll need 12½ feet (3.8 m) of wire fencing, but the basic steps remain the same.

MATERIALS NEEDED:
- Gloves
- Tape measure
- 10 feet (3 m) wire fencing, 3 feet (90 cm) tall
- Tin snips
- Zip ties

SPACE NEEDED: Less than 3 × 3 feet (90 × 90 cm)
TIME NEEDED: Less than ½ hour

LET'S DO IT

STEP 1. Wearing gloves, measure out 10 feet (3 m) of wire fencing. Galvanized steel is easy to work with and stays sturdy and straight in the backyard.

Measure at least 10 feet (3 m) of fencing to form a 3-foot (90-cm) bin. You will overlap some of the fencing to create strength.

Use tin snips to cut the fence to the right size, at least 10 feet (3 m) in length.

Secure the bin with zip ties or other fastener you have on hand.

STEP 1. Use tin snips to cut the fencing as near the intersections as possible so that little metal spikes don't snag your clothes or skin. Wear gloves and cut carefully, as this metal can be sharp.

STEP 2. Form the wire fencing into a circle 3 feet (90 cm) in diameter. The fencing will overlap and add strength to the final bin.

STEP 3. Use zip ties to secure the overlapping fencing to itself.

STEP 4. Place the bin where you want it and fill it up with leaves.

Fill your fence bin with leaves for the easiest type of composting.

To harvest a leaf bin, simply lift the bin off the leaves, remove the leaves from the outside that are not quite finished decomposing, and scoop up your gorgeous compost. Soil scientists and gardeners refer to finished compost made mostly of leaves as "leaf mold." Although leaf mold does not have the high values of nitrogen and other nutrients that traditional compost contains, it has a fantastic texture that helps amend soils and improve water retention for your plants.

HOW TO SPEED UP LEAF COMPOSTING

Leaves will obviously decompose without your assistance, but depending on the species, the process may take several years. With a few tricks, you can turn fall leaves into spring compost.

First, shred the leaves. This may require running over them with a lawnmower or going at them with a weed trimmer. If you want an afternoon of real fun, buy or rent a leaf mulcher, which acts like a small chipper shredder but only for leaves. Once the leaves are smaller, the macro- and microorganisms can break them down much faster.

Next, add a high-nitrogen material, preferably coffee grounds. Most animals dislike the smell of coffee grounds, so you won't attract unwanted guests as you would with other food scraps, but you will receive the benefit of the nitrogen to help break down the high-carbon leaves. Layering the coffee grounds in the leaves as you pile them up is more effective than just throwing the coffee grounds on top. Many local coffee shops will gladly share their spent coffee grounds with gardeners and composters, so you can access bulk grounds without brewing enough coffee for an army.

One last tip: Add urine to the leaf pile. Urine is high in available liquid nitrogen and acts immediately to help decompose the leaves. Of course, use discretion in how the urine gets to the pile. Direct application may result in a few raised eyebrows from onlooking neighbors.

Spent coffee grounds and leaves make beautiful compost when mixed together.

Integrate Composting into Your Garden

||||||||||||||||||||||||||||||||||||||

THINKING OUTSIDE OF THE BIN

Many urban and suburban composters choose to compost in a contained bin because it offers the benefits of holding all your organics in a neat, controlled package. If you have a little more space or some creativity, you can integrate your composting efforts into your garden or landscaping. Once you escape the confines of your bin, you are free to compost as much material as you want. Let's check out a few tried-and-true techniques.

PIT AND TRENCH COMPOSTING

Many people living in a homeowner's association or community that prohibits composting choose this method for composting on the down-low. Burying your food scraps under the ground keeps above ground critters out of your pile while bringing the food scraps to the worms' front door. This technique also hides the evidence and masks all odors associated with decomposing scraps. As an added bonus, once everything you bury decomposes into compost, the material is already integrated into your garden—no need to harvest compost or work the material into the soil.

Underground composting will likely go anaerobic at some point. As anyone who has had the nightmare of being buried alive knows, the air will eventually run out. Because the material is underground, however, you only need a good layer of soil on top and patience. The soil will mask odors, and given enough time, your material will decompose.

The best places to integrate underground composting are rows in a vegetable garden or a landscaping bed you want to replenish for next year. Pit and trench composting improve soil with little humus material, such as heavy clay or sandy soil, adding nutrients and improving soil structure right in the root zone of plants.

You can "sneak" pit composting into an existing garden bed that needs a replenish. Search for spots without plants where you may want to plant next year.

Pit composting allows you to amend poor soil while making your composting invisible to neighbors.

Trench composting can be adapted to the size of your yard and how often you want to add food scraps. The only difference between pit and trench composting is the shape. You can think of pit composting as a circular hole in the ground. Trench composting looks more like a rectangle. After you try a few methods, you may develop your own technique that works best for your lifestyle.

PIT COMPOSTING

Pit composting involves digging a hole at least 1 foot (30 cm) deep (up to 2 feet [60 cm] if you are in a digging mood) and filling it 4 to 6 inches (10 to 15 cm) with food scraps and leaves. Fill the remainder of the hole with the soil you removed. Pit composting is less organized than trench composting; usually you just bring a few days' worth of scraps out to your garden, dig a hole, drop the scraps, and bury them. Think of it as the "dig and drop" method.

The hardest part of pit composting, if you can even call it "hard," is remembering where you dug your pits so you don't dig it up before the material decomposes. If this idea troubles you, mark the piles with old popsicle sticks or some other marker. You could even get really organized and date the sticks so you know when you buried the material.

Choose an area of the garden not currently in use. As the materials decompose, they temporarily draw nitrogen out of the surrounding soil, and that could affect a sensitive plant nearby.

PIT COMPOSTING

IIIIIIIIIIIIIIIIIIIIIIIIIIIIIIIIIIII

Pit composting works best in beds you intend to plant next year that need a little more humus material.

MATERIALS NEEDED:

▶ Shovel

▶ Popsicle stick or other marker

▶ Strong back

SPACE NEEDED: 1 × 1 feet (30 × 30 cm) per pit

TIME NEEDED: 15 minutes

Start pit or trench composting by digging down about 1 foot (30 cm).

Fill the bottom of the hole with food scraps and brown leaves.

LET'S DO IT

STEP 1. Dig a pit at least 1 foot (30 cm) deep.

STEP 2. Fill the bottom of the pit with 4 to 6 inches (10 to 15 cm) of food scraps and leaves.

STEP 3. Fill the rest of the pit with soil. Mark the location with a popsicle stick. Wait 6 months to a year before planting over the top.

Cover your pit or trench with at least 5 inches (13 cm) of soil and wait at least 6 months to plant in the area.

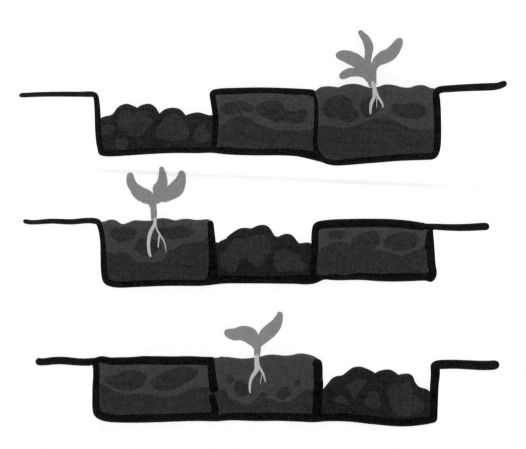

Simple garden row trenches amend your soil while allowing you to easily garden at the same time.

SIMPLE GARDEN ROW TRENCHES

If you have a garden with rows, organize your trench composting into two stages. During one season, dig your trenches and bury the scraps and leaves between the rows, where you walk. This allows the scraps many months to a year to decompose before you plant again. The next year, plant in your now-amended trench rows and add scraps to the rows you planted in the previous year. Rotating the trenches amends the soil and gives you an easy method to keep track of your trench composting.

DEEPER TRENCH

Another method involves digging a deeper trench of 18 to 24 inches (45 to 60 cm). This method makes the most sense when you have very poor soil in need of amendment.

DEEP TRENCH COMPOSTING

||||||||||||||||||||||||||||||||||

When determining where you want to locate your trench, dig a small hole to make sure there are not a lot of rocks in the area that would slow down the trench-digging process. If after a few tries you only find rock-filled soil, you may have to accept your lot in life and get to work on the rocks.

MATERIALS NEEDED:
- Shovel
- Tarp or cardboard (optional)
- Temporary protective barrier (optional)

SPACE NEEDED: 6 × 3 feet (1.8 m × 90 cm)
TIME NEEDED: 1 to 3 hours (depending on your soil and how many breaks you take)

LET'S DO IT

STEP 1. Dig a deep trench that measures at least 18 inches (45 cm). Most deep trenches have lengths of 4 to 6 feet (1.2 to 1.8 m), about long enough to lay down in. If you lay a piece of cardboard or a tarp down next to the trench to scoop the soil onto, you will have an easier time moving the soil back on top of the food waste.

STEP 2. Add food scraps to the trench and layer with leaves and other compostables, such as plant trimmings.

STEP 3. Cover with 1 inch (2.5 cm) of soil. Temporarily cover the trench with a protective barrier, such as fencing, if needed.

STEP 4. Continue this layering over a few weeks until you have filled within 5 inches (13 cm) of the top.

STEP 5. Fill the top 5 inches (13 cm) with soil and mound more soil over the top to allow for settling.

STEP 6. Wait 6 months to 1 year before planting on top of the trench.

The deeper trench method allows you to do more digging at one time and then use the same trench for a few weeks. Depending on the soil conditions and bedrock where you live, digging 18 inches (45 cm) into the ground with only a shovel may prove difficult. Only attempt to dig a trench in unfrozen soil. Too many rocks or too much impenetrable clay may require an aerobic workout and a sharp shovel to break through, but the end result of more fertile soil for your plants is worth a little sweat.

||||||||||||||||||||||||||||||||||

What to Expect with Trench Composting
Because this type of composting technically falls under the cold composting category and is often anaerobic, your materials will take longer to decompose than with a hotter method. Depending on the type of food scraps you place in your pit or trench, the organisms in the soil, the season, and your climate, what you bury will become unrecognizable in 6 months. In

KEEPING CRITTERS OUT OF YOUR DEEP TRENCH

Topping your pit or trench with 5 inches (13 cm) of topsoil should discourage most nosy animal neighbors from digging into your compost. However, the deep trench method has only 1 inch (2.5 cm) of soil over food scraps for an extended period, sometimes a few weeks. If you know that raccoons, squirrels, or even dogs frequent your yard, you may need additional fortification to protect your compost.

After adding the 1 inch (2.5 cm) of soil, you could temporarily cover the area with chicken wire or another type of fencing you have on hand. You could even use thick cardboard for the job. Weight down the two sides with rocks or something else too heavy for our furry friends to lift. Look around and get creative. I spoke with one gardener who covered his garden trench with an old heavy door until he was finished adding food scraps.

Aside from a physical barrier, you could place an olfactory barrier. Covering the soil with a layer of coffee grounds will add to the compost and deter some animals. Ammonia also acts as an olfactory deterrent. Most wild animals (and most humans) dislike the stringent smell of ammonia. You can place a small open container of ammonia on the pile or tie strips of rags soaked in ammonia nearby. Ammonia does burn plants, though, so be careful not to allow the ammonia to touch plant leaves.

a warm, wetter climate or season with small scraps you may find they disappear in a month or two. This is cold composting; it takes longer because the microbial activity is lower and the compost generally doesn't heat up. One easy way to check—get out the shovel and dig in.

Pit and trench composting work well in sandy soil because the water in food scraps can easily drain away. These methods also do well in hot, dry climates where composters face difficulties keeping their above-ground compost piles moist enough. However, composters with all types of soil can enjoy the benefits of underground composting; some may need a sharper shovel and a stronger back.

Even though this composting takes place underground, you still need to watch the carbon and nitrogen mix of materials. Only adding food scraps will result in slower decomposition than also adding dry leaves or other brown materials.

Usually wait a year to plant material on top of your pit or trench. High-carbon material will call upon the nitrogen reserves in the soil to decompose. Conversely, the high-nitrogen materials may release the wrong form of nitrogen right away. Waiting to plant for a year will make sure the material properly decomposes, making the nitrogen available for plants. If you must plant on top of the trench, add bone meal or blood meal to the pile before you cover with soil to give a nitrogen boost.

One downside of underground composting is that the material may not get hot enough to kill seeds in the food scraps or plants you add. You may notice peppers and tomato plants coming up from your rotten vegetables. If volunteer plants bother you, try digging the trench even deeper. Most seeds buried at least 1 foot (30 cm) deep will eventually decompose with no hope of sprouting to the surface.

AFRICAN KEYHOLE GARDEN

Finished compost provides your garden with numerous benefits, but what if you could also reap benefits from your compost while the pile decomposes? African keyhole gardens place composting in the center of a small-scale raised bed. The plants in the bed benefit from the nutrient-rich runoff coming from the pile and the increase in macro- and microorganisms drawn by the compost. The compost benefits from the insulation of the bed and the shared organisms. Everyone is happy and everyone wins, including you.

Construction of African keyhole gardens is limited only by your imagination. Most gardeners building them use found or leftover materials, including bricks, rocks, and pavers. The key is to create a raised bed with a compost bin in the center. Ideally the compost bin is made from wire or mesh, allowing easy transfer of moisture and organisms with the surrounding soil.

As the name implies, African keyhole gardens originated in Africa as a way to intensively grow vegetables in a manner that retains moisture and reduces the need for watering. Anyone in a hot or dry climate will benefit from building one of these gardens, but raised garden beds offer benefits we can all appreciate.

◀ The compost bin in the center of an African keyhole garden provides nutrients and water to the surrounding bed.

▼ This finished African keyhole garden will provide water and nutrients to plants in the raised bed.

AFRICAN KEYHOLE GARDEN

||||||||||||||||||||||||||||||||||

Instead of creating a perfectly circular garden bed, notch the circle with a keyhole to give access to the compost bin in the center. That way you can easily walk up to the compost and deposit materials without needing to reach over a garden bed.

MATERIALS NEEDED:

- ▸ Gloves
- ▸ Shovel
- ▸ String or measuring tool
- ▸ Compost bin for center (wire fencing works well)

- ▸ Material for outside wall (e.g., brick, stone, wood, etc.)
- ▸ Soil
- ▸ Creativity

SPACE NEEDED: 6 × 6 feet (1.8 × 1.8 m)

TIME NEEDED: 4 hours

LET'S DO IT

STEP 1. First, wearing gloves, clear an area for the bed and measure two circles. The first inner circle will be the composting area and should measure between 1 and 3 feet (30 to 90 cm) in diameter. The outer circle should measure 6 feet (1.8 m) in diameter.

STEP 2. Notch the outer circle with a keyhole patch large enough for you to access the compost in the center.

STEP 3. Create the compost basket or bin first. A simple wire mesh cylinder works perfectly. I've seen people in Uganda expertly weaving the inner compost basket from strong bamboo-like poles and bendable branches. Use materials to which you have easy access. Remember that soil will surround this bin, so it needs to be strong enough to withstand the weight. If you use wire mesh, reinforce the mesh with vertical pieces of wood to support the weight or loop the mesh into multiple layers to increase the strength.

Create a "keyhole" or notch to give easy access to the central compost bin.

Traditionally, builders of African keyhole gardens line the bottom and sides of the bed with a thick layer of cardboard or other water-resistant material before adding soil. The layer acts to hold in water in hot, dry climates but is unnecessary in temperate regions. You can also layer sticks in the bottom for drainage and a little Hügelkultur action (see next project).

STEP 4. Once a sturdy bin is ready, build the outside wall. You can use bricks, stones, pavers, or pretty much any material you can stack in a circle to create a bed. We used logs from a tree cut down recently. This African keyhole garden will only last a few years before the wood degrades. If you want a longer lasting bin, use stone, concrete, metal, or plastic materials.

OPTIONAL: Line the sides with landscaping fabric or straw if your outside wall will allow soil to seep through.

STEP 5. Fill the compost bin with material first to further increase the strength of the bin. You can add all the same materials you would add to a regular backyard composting setup.

STEP 6. Fill in the surrounding bed with soil and finished compost.

STEP 7. Plant what your heart desires. Many African keyhole gardens contain vegetables, but you could plant flowers, herbs, or any smaller landscaping plant you choose. When the bed needs watering, water the center compost bin and allow the water to trickle down to the rest of the bed.

Some African keyhole gardens have modest walls, while others stretch 3 feet (90 cm) high or taller. The height depends on your landscape and resources. A taller outside wall will allow you to fill the bed with more soil and reap more benefit from the interior compost bin. I've seen shorter outside walls holding in a small mound of soil with the peak of the hill cresting at the compost pile.

Depending on the depth of your African keyhole garden bed, you will occasionally need to dig out the finished compost from the inner bin. For most setups, digging out the material once per year will prove sufficient.

Wire fencing creates a durable inner compost bin that will allow nutrients to flow out into the surrounding bed.

Add soil and compost to fill in the bed. Consider adding a layer of decomposed wood and sticks to benefit from Hügelkultur as well.

You only need to ensure you have enough space to continue adding compostables.

The compost pile in the center of an African keyhole garden provides continuous nutrients and water to the surrounding plants.

HÜGELKULTUR

Most backyard composting methods shy away from large branches and logs because they take so long to decompose. Not so with Hügelkultur composters, who use rotting logs as the basis for a raised bed supported by a mound of compost. Hügelkultur (pronounced hoo-gul-culture) uses the very gradual decay of wood to act as a long-term supply of nutrients to the plants above. People in Germany and Eastern Europe (hence the German word for "hill culture" or "mound culture") have practiced this technique for centuries, but permaculture experts recently perfected the technique and have encouraged others to take up the practice.

Gardeners using this method say that beyond nutrients, the decaying wood (and other materials) generates heat, extending the growing season for the plants. The branches and logs breaking down aerate the soil so the gardener never has to till the area. Decaying wood also acts as a sponge, soaking up water during rainy times and slowly releasing water during drier times. Most plants would appreciate this slow-release watering.

You can construct a Hügelkultur bed as a mound or in layers in a deep raised bed. And you can go as large or as small as you want to. Traditional Hügelkultur mounds are large, but most of us do not have that kind of space in our yards.

◀ Decomposing wood in a Hügelkultur mound provides the garden bed above with nutrients and water.

▼ Using wood that has started to decompose will provide immediate benefit to your Hügelkultur mound or bed.

HÜGELKULTUR BED

|||||||||||||||||||||||||||||||||||||||

Constructing a Hügelkultur bed does take some time and hard work, but reaping the benefits of the decaying material for the next twenty years seems worth the effort.

MATERIALS NEEDED:

- Cardboard
- Sharp shovel
- Hardwood and/or softwood logs and branches
- Compostable materials (grass, plant trimmings, manure, etc.)
- Compost
- Soil
- Mulch

SPACE NEEDED: At least 4 × 4 feet (1.2 × 1.2 m)

TIME NEEDED: 2 to 3 hours

LET'S DO IT

STEP 1. First, decide how large your bed will be and set out cardboard or logs to mark the area. Cardboard is helpful if you want to kill the plants under the pile.

OPTIONAL: Dig a 1-foot (30-cm)-deep trench the size of your bed. The bed can measure any length and width you choose. This gives your mound more decomposing material without getting too tall. If you have very difficult to dig soil or a high water table (or you are just a little lazy like me) you can skip this step with no problem.

STEP 2. Start with a layer of hardwood on the bottom and then with softwood if you have both. The hardwoods will decay more slowly and the softwoods more quickly, so a mix is nice, but any wood combination will work. Avoid black walnut and black locust because they release potentially toxic chemicals (for your plants) as they decompose.

STEP 3. Continue building the mound with any bulky organic material you would like to compost. Adding some well-rotted wood

Build your Hügelkultur mound using a combination of larger and smaller pieces of wood. Invite neighbors and make it a social event.

Tuck leaves and other traditional compostables into open spaces and layer over the top of the more woody material.

Add a layer of soil to cover the mound. Some of the larger logs at the base can be left exposed if you like the look.

You can plant or seed your Hügelkultur mound right away, or let it rest and settle first.

in there will help the new wood decompose faster and provide nutrients to your plants sooner. Remember, you can break the rules with Hügelkultur. Tough roots, shrubs, and vines are all fair game. Every once in a while, walk on the mound to make it more compact and decrease how much it will settle.

STEP 1. Over the tougher materials, add more traditional compostables such as leaves, straw, and manure. You can mound as high as you would like.

STEP 2. Cover your materials with a 1-inch (2.5-cm) layer of finished compost and a few inches (5 to 7.5 cm) of topsoil. Work the compost and soil into the air pockets around the pile so your finished mound has a smooth shape. Add a layer of mulch to protect the soil.

STEP 3. Either allow your pile to rest for a time before planting (it will settle) or plant seeds or starter plants on the mound. Roots from plants will help secure the soil on the mound.

Hügelkultur beds work well in areas with very poor soil where you are "starting from scratch" as far as building up a garden. Gardeners who prefer not to water a bed regularly will also find a benefit in the slow-release, sponge-like rotting wood under the bed. These beds look like a mound and they add some interesting height to your garden, which could spice up your landscaping.

Raised Bed Hügelkultur

Adding a Hügelkultur mound under your raised bed saves you money and provides slow-release water and nutrients to plants in the raised bed. This works best if you have a deeper raised bed so you still have room for soil on top or if you dig down underneath your raised bed to have a "pit" for your Hügelkultur.

Follow the same steps as a mound but do them in the bottom of your raised bed. Layer cardboard, a combination of rotting and newer wood, softwood and hardwood, sticks, and

This raised bed contains layers of wood, sticks, and compost to create a Hügelkultur raised bed.

Layer hardwoods, softwoods, leaves, and other compostables, leaving about 12 inches (30 cm) on top for your garden soil. These materials will slowly decompose, providing nutrients and moisture to the plants above.

manure or compost in the bottom. Rather than forming a mound, you are layering the materials into a flat surface like a lasagna. Walk on the layers every once in a while, to help flatten. Fill the top of the bed with 8 to 12 inches (20 to 30 cm) of soil mixed with finished compost. Because you have so much soil on top, you can plant immediately.

Have you priced out buying good garden soil? You can fork over a pretty penny trying to fill up a raised bed with just soil. And you don't need more than 12 inches (30 cm) of soil in your raised bed. Next time you create a raised bed, consider sneaking in some logs and sticks at the bottom and save the money you would have spent on soil to buy more plants. If you are like me, you can always use more plants.

Would You, Could You, Use This Wood?

Not all woods work equally well with Hügelkultur, so I've pulled together a table to use as a guide. When using varieties listed in the "Okay" column, only add them when they're well rotted or aged so they do not sprout and are less likely to release antimicrobial chemicals. Most species in this column have a strong resistance to decay, meaning they will last in your mound for a long time. Those species in the "Avoid" column include black locust, which will not decompose in your lifetime; black walnut, which contains the plant-toxic chemical juglone; and old-growth redwoods, which have persistent chemicals that can prevent seed germination.

Wood Selection for Hügelkultur

BEST	OKAY	AVOID
Alder	Black cherry	Black locust
Apple	Camphor	Black walnut
Aspen	Cedar	Old-growth
Birch	Eucalyptus	redwood
Cottonwood	Fir	
Maple	Honeysuckle	
Oak	Juniper	
Poplar	Osage orange	
	Pacific yew	
	Pine or spruce	
	Red mulberry	
	Willow	

HOT COMPOSTING

Think of hot composting as graduate-level composting. Hot composting is a technique governing what you put in and how you maintain compost that is, frankly, a lot of work but results in super-fast finished compost. This method, also called batch composting or active composting, employs every possible advantage to create the optimal environment for microbial activity within a compost pile. That microbial activity generates heat, causing the pile to increase in temperature and rapidly decompose.

People using hot composting techniques, we'll call them hot composters, generate finished compost in as little as 3 weeks.

Hot Composting Materials

Hot composting requires that you add all your materials at once, rather than over the weeks and months you naturally generate the materials. This means you will need to freeze a month's worth of kitchen scraps, run to your local coffee shop for a donation of used grounds, and stockpile your leaves and yard trimmings until you have enough to make a large pile.

All materials you add to a hot compost pile should be chopped or ground as small as possible. You can't add a whole pumpkin or even a whole stalk of celery. Keeping everything smaller than 2 inches (5 cm) will increase surface area and speed up decomposition. Branches and unchipped wood have no place in a hot compost pile.

You also need to perfectly balance the carbon and nitrogen in your pile. Add three parts brown for every one part green. Traditional composting allows you more variation in brown versus green, but the 3:1 ratio must be perfect for hot composting to work.

OPTIONAL HOT COMPOSTING STRUCTURE

You do not need a structure for hot composting, but if you want to designate an area of your yard for composting, having a structure with "bays" for the compost makes your composting effort look much more organized. Your significant other or neighbor may be more impressed with your composting if it appears more official than just a pile of rotting stuff under a tarp.

Imagine you are hovering over the structure from above like a bee. When you look down, your composting structure will resemble an "E." Hot composting structures forgo the walls on the front to allow easy access for turning. You will move the material between the two bays each time you turn the pile.

HOT COMPOSTING PILE

||||||||||||||||||||||||||||||||||||

It is not necessary to have a structure because hot composting happens so fast. Not having a structure actually makes hot composting easier. Choose a spot out of the way but near enough to your garden that you can effortlessly use the finished compost where you need it most.

MATERIALS NEEDED:

▶ Cardboard or straw
▶ Balance of brown and green materials
▶ Finished compost
▶ Pitchfork
▶ Water
▶ Tarp (or hot composting bay)

SPACE NEEDED: 4 × 4 feet (1.2 × 1.2 m)
TIME NEEDED: 1 hour

LET'S DO IT

STEP 1. Start with a layer of cardboard and/or straw to improve airflow in the pile. Also, when you go to turn the compost pile or harvest the finished compost, finding the bottom of the pile becomes easier with the cardboard underneath. If you don't have straw, your pile will work just fine. We used moldy hay unsuitable for animals to eat in place of straw.

STEP 2. As you build the pile, the easiest way to ensure a good ratio is to add the brown and green materials in thin layers that can easily mix.

Any of the brown and green materials listed in chapter 2 (page 25) can build your hot composting pile. Some materials break down faster than others. The most common items hot composters seek:

▶ Green grass clippings (green)
▶ Herbivore manure (green)
▶ Coffee grounds (green)
▶ Food scraps in small pieces (green)
▶ Straw (brown)
▶ Shredded leaves (brown)
▶ Used herbivore animal bedding (brown)
▶ Wood chips (brown)

Add thin layers to ensure a 3:1 brown to green ratio.

Add water to the "brown" or high-carbon layers in your hot composting pile.

Adding herbivore manure or old compost halfway up the pile will inoculate the pile with beneficial microorganisms.

A finished hot composting pile should measure at least 3 feet tall and 3 feet wide (90 × 90 cm).

STEP 1. Every time you add a layer of browns, add some water to the pile. You want the composting material nice and wet, like a wrung-out sponge. If you are using wood chips, soak them in water before adding to the pile. This will ensure they are moist enough to decompose quickly and you won't end up with dry pockets in your pile.

STEP 2. Halfway up the pile, add a shovelful of old compost, herbivore manure, or another activator. Because we started on a layer of cardboard, we lose the benefit of soil organisms migrating easily into the pile. Inoculating the pile with old compost will help speed up decomposition.

STEP 3. Try to achieve a pile that measures 3 feet (90 cm) high and 3 feet (90 cm) wide. This will decrease in size as the material decomposes.

STEP 4. End with a layer of brown material, such as shredded leaves, and make sure no food scraps are visible. Cover the pile with a tarp if you have one.

Maintaining the Pile

Once built, keep a close eye on the pile to make sure it stays as wet as a wrung-out sponge. The Berkeley method of hot composting, developed by the University of California–Berkeley, requires you to leave the pile untouched for the first 4 days and then turn every other day for 14 days (turn on day 5, 7, 9, etc.). When you turn a hot compost pile, you remove the outside of the pile first and use that to create the inside of a new pile nearby. You then use the inside of the old pile to create the outside of the new pile.

The pile should maintain a temperature between 131° and 149°F (55° and 65°C). If you notice a thin layer of white fungus growing, the pile may have exceeded the desired temperature and should be turned soon.

Hot composting requires a commitment of time and energy, but if you want compost fast and have the willpower to put in the effort, you may soon call yourself a hot composter.

When turning a hot compost pile, place the outside layer on the inside to ensure even decomposition through the process.

Unique Indoor Composting Systems

||||||||||||||||||||||||||||||||||||

COMPOSTING WITHOUT A BACKYARD

More people are embracing small space living—removing the clutter and excess stuff to live a simpler life and focus on what really matters. But sometimes living in a smaller space means you do not have access to a backyard for composting. Worry not! This chapter details three methods of composting indoors or on a small terrace, balcony, or patio. All three of these methods allow you to compost food scraps in a footprint of less than 2 square feet (0.2 sq m), proving you don't need to own land to manage your own waste at home.

These methods focus on small space living and are not intended for composting materials such as leaves or brush. You can add the occasional leaf from a house plant, but these methods focus on scraps from food, such as carrot peels, onion skins, and apple cores. The three methods explained in this chapter include:

TERRA-COTTA POT COMPOSTING: Composting in terra-cotta pots has become very popular in India, where urban dwellers want to create compost in small indoor/outdoor spaces, such as a terrace or balcony. This method takes advantage of the breathability of clay to create a beautiful, stackable compost bin.

VERMICOMPOSTING: Composting with worms has been practiced by people around the world for decades. Vermicomposting puts a special type of worm, the red wiggler, to work in a small container. The worms manage their own population size and can eat half their body weight a day in food scraps.

BOKASHI: This method originated in Japan and involves fermenting your food scraps in a special container to create a precompost product. If done correctly, you can even compost materials most other composting methods cannot accept, such as meat and cheese. This section will explain Bokashi and options for using the precompost product when you finish.

Which method you choose will depend on how much space you have for composting and how interested you are in taking on 1,000 new wormy roommates.

TERRA-COTTA COMPOSTER

I will tell you a secret. This composter defies several basic "rules" of composting and by all rights should not work. But it does! The vessels measure four times smaller than most composting containers; it doesn't rely on organisms from the soil; and the compost stays much drier than I would typically recommend. I tested this rule-breaking composter in my own kitchen and it really does work. The pots even look attractive, and the terra-cotta provides airflow to the composting material to keep it drier and smelling fresh.

One problem you face when you do not have a backyard is a lack of leaves, which normally form the basis of backyard composting methods. When composting in terra-cotta pots, you use a material called cocopeat or coir as your brown carbon source. A by-product from coconut milk and coconut oil production, cocopeat comes from the fibrous coconut husk. It absorbs moisture, provides a source of carbon, and smells nice. Perhaps most important, it's widely available at a low price at home improvement stores and online.

Because this self-contained composting system does not have access to soil organisms, we will add a compost starter or effective microorganisms to the mix. These will lead to a faster, more controlled decomposition process. However, you could skip this step. Your food scraps are covered in bacteria that will eventually break down the material without help from their store-bought brethren.

This terra-cotta composter purchased online provides a decorative solution to composting food scraps in a small space.

Cover food scraps with generous amounts of cocopeat to balance the high-nitrogen food scraps and absorb excess moisture.

COCOPEAT ALTERNATIVE

If you live in a corner of the world where cocopeat is not available, you can try other materials, such as sawdust, that would balance the food scraps and absorb excess moisture. In Chile, Mimba Compost uses natural zeolites rather than importing cocopeat.

Although difficult to find in stores, these beautiful premade terra-cotta composter containers can be found online. Usually artisans handcraft these pots for the purpose of composting and include lovely decorative details. Another bonus of the premade composters is that they come with a generous supply of cocopeat already inoculated with beneficial microorganisms. As you may have suspected, given the high number of DIY projects featuring reused materials in this book, we will go step by step through building your own terra-cotta composter using old garden pots.

One of these composters lived in a corner of my kitchen for 2 months so I could test what odors it might generate. I carefully covered the food scraps with cocopeat and a layer of newspaper each day and ensured the lid fit tightly in place. It did not smell. At all. However, after 2 months, once the material really started to break down, I moved it onto a covered area of my patio. My primary reason was that decomposition without the aid of worms will inevitably involve mold and I didn't want my family exposed to mold in an indoor space. I recommend using these composters on a patio, balcony, or porch. Keep it out of the direct rain.

As you fill up the terra-cotta composter, each pot will have material at different stages of decomposition.

TERRA—COTTA COMPOSTER

|||||||||||||||||||||||||||||||||||||

The intuitive logic behind terra-cotta composters becomes simple once you stack the pots. You have a base pot and two or three filling pots with a lid on top. The base pot remains intact and always stays on the bottom. This pot stores almost-finished compost and absorbs excess moisture. The other units have holes in the bottom that allow moisture to move between pots.

MATERIALS NEEDED:

▸ 3 terra-cotta or clay pots
  (14 inches [36 cm wide])
▸ 4 terra-cotta pot saucers
  (14 inches [36 cm wide])
▸ Piece of cardboard for templates
▸ Marker or pencil
▸ Measuring tape
▸ Safety glasses
▸ Drill
▸ Masonry bit for drill (⅜ inch and ³⁄₁₆ inch)
  (also called a carbide bit)
▸ Dust mask

SPACE NEEDED: Less than 2 × 2 feet (60 × 60 cm)
TIME NEEDED: 2 hours

LET'S DO IT

I recommend stacking up your pots to better understand how they will work. If you use old pots with mismatched sizes, use the largest pot at the bottom. This pot will act as your finishing pot with an intact saucer underneath and give the structure stability.

STEP 1. Create a template to drill drain holes for two of the saucers and two of the pots. A cardboard template will make the drilling easier and give you more uniform holes. On our template we drew one hole in the middle with eight holes in a circle around that and then another circle with eight holes around that, or seventeen holes altogether.

STEP 2. Find the center of your saucer with a measuring tape. Now use your template

This terra-cotta composter looks lovely on a covered porch or terrace.

Creating a template to mark the spots before you drill will give you more uniform holes.

DRILLING TIPS

Drilling holes in terra-cotta or clay pots can be a little stressful. I think I gasped and held my breath at least a dozen times while making this and I wasn't even the one doing the drilling. Having the specialized bit for tile and natural stone can make all the difference. If you don't have that and still want to give the project a go, you can soak the pot in water and use a towel to stabilize the pot. We had no cracks or breaks though, so hopefully you will also have such luck.

Drill holes in the saucer and bottom of two of the pots to create drain holes.

and a marker or pencil and mark all of the holes on two of the saucers and the bottom of two of the pots. Wearing safety glasses and using the larger or ⅜-inch bit, start by drilling the center hole. Take it nice and easy as this is a very delicate material. This process also creates a lot of clay dust, so be ready with a broom and dustpan. Wear a dust mask while drilling to avoid breathing in the dust.

STEP 3. Now use the smaller bit (³⁄₁₆ inch) to drill air holes in the side. I wanted a decorative composter, so my husband created a pretty star pattern with one hole in the center surrounded by twenty holes to create a starburst. Repeat this pattern four times on each pot (you can see how the template makes this much easier) or until you feel like you have a good amount of airflow.

STEP 4. Stack your composting system with one undrilled saucer, the three pots (with the undrilled bottom pot first) separated by two drilled saucers, and an undrilled saucer as the lid.

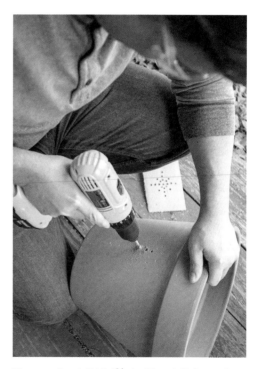

Use a smaller drill bit (³⁄₁₆ inch) to drill decorative air holes on the side of the pot using a template.

To start composting, fill the bottom pot with 4 to 6 inches (10 to 15 cm) of dried leaves and a few handfuls of cocopeat to absorb excess moisture. In the top pot, place a layer of newspaper or paper towels, a handful of cocopeat, and a teaspoon of compost starter or effective microorganisms. Add cut-up food scraps no more than once per day and cover with a few handfuls of cocopeat. Cocopeat should cover the food scraps, so use it generously. Over the cocopeat, cover with a layer of newspaper. If you don't have access to newspaper, you could use paper towel. When adding new food scraps, peel off the newspaper or paper towel and add food scraps over the top of the layer of cocopeat. Layer again with a covering of cocopeat and reuse the newspaper or paper towel until it starts to disintegrate. Try to keep food scraps very small and avoid lots of cooked vegetables, especially broccoli and cauliflower, since they tend to be smelly to start. Once per week add another teaspoon of compost starter or effective microorganisms.

Once you have almost filled the top pot, use a tool or a gloved hand to stir the material. You want a few inches of open air above the scraps. If the material is dry you can add a little water, or if it is wet, add some cocopeat. Then move the full container to the spot just above the base and start filling a fresh pot. It took my family of four about 3 weeks to fill a pot.

Once the second pot is full, empty the first pot into the base pot and start all over with the original pot. After that one is full, you can either harvest the material in the base pot or add material from pot two into the base pot. During harvest, screen the material from the base pot to pull out any large items. You should have material ready to harvest in about 2 to 3 months. If you find you fill up pots faster than the system can handle, add another pot.

After 2 months the food scraps in this terra-cotta composter are almost fully decomposed.

Terra–Cotta Pot Compostables

WHAT TO ADD
Fresh fruit peels and cores
Fresh vegetable scraps
Small leaves from house plants
Coffee grounds and tea leaves

WHAT TO AVOID
Cooked vegetables or grains
Yard trimmings (except a few leaves)
Animal manure

VERMICOMPOSTING

Imagine if you could keep hundreds, even thousands, of pets in your home that would happily live in a container small enough to fit under your sink. Now imagine these pets were useful for more than just cuddling. They eat your table scraps without a fuss, and their poop, rather than being a gross by-product, is actually one of the best soil amendments in the world.

Vermicomposting (also called worm bin composting or vermiculture) is a special kind of composting you can do inside your home rather than in your backyard. When you get past the ick factor of keeping worms, the process is quite clean. No odors, no turning the compost, and the vermicasts created by the worms look a lot like coffee grounds.

Some people choose to vermicompost because they don't like going out to their backyard bin in the winter or they live in an apartment with no backyard. Others like the convenience of composting food scraps indoors and use their backyard bin for yard trimmings and leaves. Still others enjoy maintaining a worm bin with their children as a way to learn about biology and decomposition in nature.

These small, red wigglers can eat half their weight in food scraps every day.

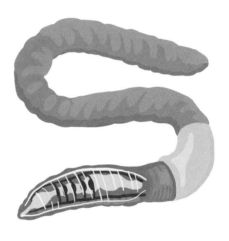

With amazingly simple anatomy, small but mighty worms can help decompose incredible volumes of material.

Vermi Wormy

You cannot dig a few earthworms out of the ground, throw them into a box, and call it a worm bin. Vermicomposting systems demand a special worm: *Eisenia fetida*, or red wigglers. These little red worms like living in shallow containers, consume a large amount of food scraps in a short time, tolerate a wide range of temperatures, and reproduce quickly when provided a nice habitat and continuous supply of food. Once adjusted to your worm bin, red wigglers can process half of their body weight in fruit and vegetable scraps every day. The average-size bin holds a pound (454 g) of worms, and you could feed your worms a half pound (227 g) of food scraps every day. Not so coincidently, this capacity generally takes care of the scraps from a family of four.

The worms eat the food scraps and produce vermicastings (worm poop). This high-nitrogen manure mixes with other decaying matter in the worm bin to create vermicompost.

Gardeners prize vermicompost for its nutrient-rich humus texture, and those without worm bins pay a pretty penny to use it as a soil amendment and fertilizer.

Creating a Mini Ecosystem

Although red wigglers are the stars of the show, they have a strong support network of other decomposers that help break down the food scraps. Your worm bin is a mini ecosystem containing a whole food web of organisms. Food scraps and other organic matter fuel the system.

Single-cell bacteria and fungi offer the chief assistance for our worms. In fact, you can consider earthworms to be microbe farmers, creating an environment perfect for these helpful creatures. The digestive tract of the worms spans almost the entire length of their bodies to give bacteria the time to break down the decaying matter. Because of the microbes, what leaves the worm is actually more nutrient-rich than what entered (at least from the perspective of a plant).

Other organisms such as mold, actinomycetes (a fungus-like bacteria), beetle mites, and sow bugs will make an occasional appearance in your bin and consume the food scraps directly. Secondary consumers, such as springtails, protozoa, and feather-winged beetles, eat your first-level consumers and add to the decomposition process. You may occasionally see predators in your bin, such as centipedes, ants, and pseudoscorpians (don't worry, these "scorpions" are so tiny you can barely see them). I suggest removing any centipedes and ants you see because they may eat the "good guys."

Building Your Own Worm Bin

The containers people use for indoor worm composting vary almost as much as backyard bins. The space needs to be large enough to accommodate the colony of worms, their bedding, and food scraps and have some breathing room for good air flow. For a family of four, you generally need a box 12 to 18 inches (30 to 45 cm) deep, 2 feet (60 cm) wide, and 3 feet (90 cm) long.

The selection of premade worm bins on the market today come with clever brand names such as Worm Wigwam, VermiHut, and Worm Factory. Some of these bins offer nice features designed to improve ease of harvesting the compost and adding the food scraps. If you want to splurge on a high-rise condo for your worms, I suggest reading the reviews of the particular model you desire. The function of premade bin features come with varying levels of success.

You can also build your own worm bin using plywood or a plastic storage container. Basically, a worm bin is a box with holes, a lid, and a way for liquids to drain. You can find plans for wood bins, but the container will remain moist most of the time, so a plastic bin will last longer. A shallow container between 12 and 18 inches (30 to 45 cm) deep works best because the bedding tends to compact in a deep container.

PLASTIC STORAGE BIN VERMICOMPOSTER

||||||||||||||||||||||||||||||||||||||

Making your own worm bin is super simple and a fun project to do with kids. The plans use a plastic container, and you need to drill lots of air holes and drain holes to make sure your worm friends have plenty of ventilation and excess moisture can escape. You can order red wigglers online or sometimes find them in a bait shop. Just make sure you are getting the right species (*Eisenia fetida*) or you could end up with worms that try to escape or simply die because they cannot survive in this type of container.

Bedding choices include shredded newspaper, shredded cardboard, animal manure, leaf mold compost, or peat moss. You could run newspaper (black and white only) through a paper shredder or, even better, task your kid helpers with ripping the papers by hand. Adding a few handfuls of shredded leaves will improve the appearance of the finished vermicompost, but it may also introduce predators, such as centipedes.

Red wigglers are naturally litter dwellers, so they don't tunnel through the soil like traditional earthworms. They prefer the shredded-paper-and-food-scrap habitat we create in the bin. You do need to add a handful of good living garden soil when preparing the bin to add grit. The worms do not have teeth and they use this grit in their gizzards to help break down the food scraps. This soil also inoculates the bin with bacteria, mold, and fungi to help in the composting process.

MATERIALS NEEDED:
- Large bowl or bucket
- Water
- 1 plastic storage container (about 10 gallons [38 L]; do not use clear)
- Drill
- 2 plastic storage container lids
- Shredded newspaper (about 5 pounds [2.3 kg])
- 1 cup (128 g) soil
- 1 pound (454 g) red wigglers (*Eisenia fetida*)
- 4 bricks or blocks of wood

SPACE NEEDED: 2 × 2 feet (60 × 60 cm)

TIME NEEDED: 1 hour

Shredded newspaper makes the best bedding for worm bins because it holds moisture and is readily available.

Drill about twenty drain holes in the bottom of the bin and holes around the top of the bin for ventilation.

Add soaked and wrung-out shredded newspaper as your bedding to fill the bin three-quarters full. It will take more paper than you think.

LET'S DO IT

STEP 1. Fill a large bowl or small bucket with water and set it aside for a few hours to allow the chlorine to evaporate (or pull water from your rain barrel).

STEP 2. Turn the bin over and drill eighteen to twenty ¼-inch (6 mm) holes in the bottom of the worm bin for drainage. Space the drainage holes about 2 inches (5 cm) apart.

STEP 3. Create ventilation holes in the plastic bin by drilling ¼-inch (6-mm) holes along the top side of the bin. Keep the holes about 2 inches (5 cm) apart. Don't worry about the worms escaping; if you use the correct species and maintain the bin, these worms will happily stay inside.

STEP 4. Choose one lid to act as the lid of the bin (the other will act as the tray under the bin). Drill more ventilation holes around the lid of the bin, about 2 inches (5 cm) apart. About fifteen to twenty holes will work.

Remember, the worms need air, but they also prefer a dark environment. Too many holes will bring in too much light and hurt their little worm eyes (really, light receptors; worms do not have eyes).

STEP 5. Now gather your bedding material. I prefer shredded newspaper with a few handfuls of brown leaves. Soak the newspaper in the bowl or bucket of water you set aside in step 1 until the pieces are saturated. Lift out the paper and wring it out until no longer dripping. You will need enough bedding to fill the bin three-quarters full. It will take more newspaper than you think: about ½ pound (227 g) for every gallon (3.6 L) capacity of your bin.

STEP 6. Transfer your soaked and wrung-out newspaper to the worm bin. Mix in soil and leaves, if desired, until the materials are evenly distributed.

STEP 7. Introduce the worms by gently spreading them out in the bin. Welcome home, wormies!

STEP 8. Now, add some food scraps to the bin. The smaller the pieces are, the faster they will break down. Start with ¼ pound (113 g) of food scraps.

STEP 9. Cover all the food scraps with bedding to avoid fruit flies.

STEP 10. Set the undrilled lid onto your work surface to act as a leachate tray. Place a spacer material, such as a few bricks or blocks of wood, between the bin and leachate tray. These spacers hold the bin up off the leachate tray, allowing for drainage and air flow. Rest the bin on the spacers.

Gently add your worms to the bedding material and their new home.

||||||||||||||||||||||||||||||||||||||||||

Taking Care of Your New Pets

Although you are unlikely to name the 1,000+ new housemates, they are live animals that require some basic needs to thrive. You will need to consider the following:

TEMPERATURE: Keep your worm bin at a temperature between 55° and 77°F (13° and 25°C). Because the bedding is wet, it can freeze more easily than the surrounding air. Temperatures below 50°F (10°C) will significantly slow down the worm activity. Temperatures above 84°F (29°C) will likely prove fatal to the worms. The best places to store your worms to avoid the temperature extremes tend to be non-drafty basements or garages or, if you can convince the rest of your family, right under the kitchen sink.

VENTILATION: Worms "breathe" through their skin and create carbon dioxide and other gases like any living organism. They must have fresh air, or they will eventually smother and die. Provide plenty of air holes in the bin and never wrap the bin in a plastic bag. When you add the food scraps, fluff up the bedding to circulate the air in the bin.

MOISTURE: We added water to the bedding because worms need to keep their skin wet in order to "breathe" or exchange air. Too much water will drown the worms, though, so keep an eye on the moisture and maintain a wrung-out sponge level of dampness in the bin.

ACIDITY: Worms can survive a fairly wide range of pH, between 5 and 9. (Neutral pH is 7.) Be careful not to add anything too acidic, such as lots of lemon peels, or you could bring the acidity to dangerous levels. Often, if you see worms trying to escape the bin, the habitat is too acidic or too wet.

Worms may seem like high-maintenance pets, but once you have these basics down, the worms are fairly easy to keep alive. You can leave a worm bin untouched for a few weeks and go back to worms still munching away. If you intend to vacation for a month or more, I recommend boarding your worms with a sympathetic friend.

Feeding Your Worms

Worms will eat any kitchen scraps you have, but start with fresh fruit and vegetable scraps as a novice vermicomposter. Chopping up dense scraps, such as broccoli stems, will make munching easier for your worms. Start by adding these basic scraps:

- Potato peels
- Banana peels
- Outside leaves from lettuce and cabbage
- Celery ends

- Onion peels
- Apple and pear cores
- Tea leaves
- Coffee grounds
- Tomato stems

You get the idea. Any parts left over from cutting fruits and vegetables. Spent coffee grounds and tea leaves also make easy additions. If you have 1 pound (454 g) of worms, you can add up to a half pound (227 g) of food a day—think five banana peels or half a head of lettuce.

Just as when you backyard compost, you must bury food scraps after you add them. This will keep fruit flies from laying eggs on scraps at the surface or hatching if the larvae are already on your food. I keep a garden fork near the worm bin and simply lift a layer of bedding before dumping the scraps.

You can experiment with most food, but there are a few types of scraps you should not add to your bin.

- Meat and bones: Meat creates foul odors as it decomposes and attracts unwanted guests to the bin.

- Citrus peels: A few are okay, but citrus peels can lower the pH of the bin and also seem to attract little white mites. I avoid these completely but know some vermicomposters who add citrus in moderation.

- Dog and cat feces: Manure from your non-worm pets will stink and will also add harmful pathogens to the final compost.

Feed your new worm friends with fresh food scraps. They can eat half their body weight in food scraps a day.

HARVESTING YOUR VERMICOMPOST

|||||||||||||||||||||||||||||||||||

There are two schools of thought when it comes to harvesting vermicompost. Some people choose the "lazy route," which involves, as you might expect, less work, but you will lose most, if not all, of your worms. You can feed your worms for a period of time (at least 6 months) and then stop feeding them altogether. If you leave the worm bin unattended for a few months, the worms will eat all the food scraps, stop reproducing, and eventually starve to death and die, becoming part of your vermicompost. You will then have a container full of finished vermicompost you can use, but you will have to buy more worms to start a new bin.

If you prefer a less-macabre method of harvesting vermicompost, you will need to separate the worms from the compost. This is a more time-intensive process than harvesting backyard compost, but the payoff is worth the effort. I have harvested vermicompost using multiple techniques, and the following steps involve the least work for the greatest reward. You will know your bin is ready to harvest when you see lots of dark brown vermicompost that looks like heaps of coffee grounds.

MATERIALS NEEDED:

- Ready-to-harvest worm bin
- Plastic mesh bag filled with food scraps
- 2 buckets, one with a cover
- Tarp
- Light source (sun preferred)
- Hand shovel or garden trowel
- Garden gloves

SPACE NEEDED: 3 × 3 feet (90 × 90 cm) minimum

TIME NEEDED: 2 hours separating, 2 weeks for whole process

LET'S DO IT

STEP 1. Take a plastic mesh bag that formerly held produce such as oranges and potatoes. Fill the bag with food scraps and bury the bag on one side of the bin.

STEP 2. Wait about 2 weeks and most of your wormies will have migrated to that side of the bin. Do not add food scraps anywhere else during those few weeks.

STEP 3. Pull the bag out (with a few hundred hanging worms) and place it in a temporary holding bucket. Cover the bucket to make the area dark and keep the worms happy.

STEP 4. Now you have a bin with most of the worms removed, but some will still be left. Spread out a tarp and create cone-shaped piles of your vermicompost on the tarp.

This works best outside on a sunny day. The light-adverse worms will travel to the bottom of the piles. Be patient; the worms are slow.

STEP 5. While you wait for the worms to migrate, start your next bin with some fresh, moist bedding and leaves, following the steps earlier in this chapter (page 85). Add the worms lured by the food bag into their new home.

STEP 6. After 30 minutes or more, the remaining worms will have all migrated deeper into the cone-shaped piles. You can scrape off the tops of the cones using a shovel (or your hands) into a bucket. Shape the now-topless piles into new cones and wait again.

These lettuce seedlings grew faster with the help of vermicompost.

Eventually, I grow tired of the cone shaping and decide to just get in there and finish the process. I have a leave-no-man-behind attitude when it comes to harvesting vermicompost. This requires a few hours of quiet contemplation as I sift through the remainder of the compost and is a perfect time to catch up on a favorite podcast or audiobook.

Wearing gloves, I pick up the worms and worm cocoons (little amber-colored balls the size of a match head) and gently toss them into the new bin. I go through each pile, spreading out the compost and picking up the little wiggly friends. What is left behind I happily scoop into my harvest bucket.

At any point in the cone-scrape-shape method, you could decide to just toss the remaining vermicompost and worms back into your "new" bin (gently!). A little of the finished vermicompost actually helps jump-start your new bin with microbes.

To harvest compost in the winter or on a rainy day, you could set up a table with a tarp in your basement for the harvest. You will need a bright light—or a few—to mimic the sun and encourage the worms to migrate lower in your cone-shaped piles.

A nice bonus of this method is that you can stretch the harvesting out over several days and just go down and scrape off the tops of the cones every once in a while. Red wigglers are not native worms to most of the world. Just tossing the worms and their finished compost into your garden could introduce an alien species. The worms would likely not survive a cold winter if you have one, but it is still not worth the risk.

Using Your Worm Poop

Now that you have harvested your "black gold," you will want to reap the benefits. Vermicompost may as well be a plant superhero; it offers so many fantastic benefits.

- ▶ The spongy quality of vermicompost aerates and increases the water retention of the soil.

- ▶ In a wonder of nature, the vermicastings coming out of the worm actually have more beneficial bacteria than the food they eat or that are in the worm's gut.

- ▶ The humic acid present in the vermicompost makes nutrients and micronutrients such as calcium, iron, and potassium more readily available for plant absorption.

► Vermicompost stimulates plant growth (a perfect way to start seeds).

► The microbes present help protect plants from disease.

Give it some spandex and a cape, and vermicompost could hold a place in the Avengers lineup.

You will not have as large a quantity of compost as you do after harvesting a backyard bin. That's okay. Vermicompost is super concentrated in nutrients, and a little goes a long way.

Many vermicomposters use their compost for starting seedlings or transplanted baby plants in a vegetable garden. Simply dust a layer of vermicompost in your seed row after you have laid down the seeds. Scoop a little vermicompost into the hole you dig for a transplant. You don't need very much to make an impact.

Vermicompost also makes an excellent topdressing for houseplants and in the garden. Sprinkle some around the top of a plant and the nutrients will work their way into the soil. To use vermicompost when potting a new plant, use at least two-thirds potting soil to one-third vermicompost. You don't need more than that, so spread the love around your plants.

Troubleshooting Vermicompost Issues

PROBLEM	CAUSE	SOLUTION
Fruit flies hang around bin.	Food is not buried under bedding material.	• Bury food scraps well. • Make a fruit fly trap (see "A Quick Way to Get Rid of Fruit Flies" in chapter 2). • Hang sticky fly traps nearby. • Set the bin outside if weather permits.
Bedding dries out too quickly.	Bin has too much ventilation.	• Spray water in the bin. • Keep the lid secure. • Change the location to a less-ventilated area.
Water collects in the bottom of the bin.	Bin has poor ventilation.	• Leave the lid off for a while. • Add a little new bedding and fluff with a garden fork. • Change the location for better ventilation. • Reduce the amount of food added.
Mites are overpopulated in the bin.	A food item you placed in the bin harbored mites.	• Place a slice of white bread in the bin to attract them. The next day, pull out the white bread with all the mites and throw away.
Mold is growing in the bin.	Mold spores were on material you added.	• This isn't a big problem; you can leave it alone if you choose. • Turn the mold under material and bury it.
Bin is emitting bad odors.	• Food is not buried under bedding material. • Too many food scraps have been added. • Dairy, meat, or oily food scraps were added.	• Do not feed scraps to worms for a week. • Add dry bedding. • Bury all food scraps. • Do not add dairy or meat food scraps.

BOKASHI

If you enjoy brewing your own beer or canning your own vegetables, Bokashi might spark your interest. A Japanese method of fermenting food scraps indoors, Bokashi is more precomposting than full-cycle composting, as you have to finish composting the fermented food scraps in a backyard compost bin or by digging them into the soil. The benefits of holding food scraps in your kitchen for weeks with little odor and creating faster decomposition than traditional methods makes Bokashi worthy of consideration even if it is still a fringe composting practice in the United States.

Bokashi uses controlled anaerobic decomposition by carefully introducing the food scraps to feed beneficial microorganisms that love an anaerobic environment. Bokashi requires two things: a special bucket and inoculated bran. Although we will go over how to make a DIY bucket, you can buy a premade Bokashi bucket and the premade inoculated bran if you want to try this method.

Start your Bokashi by placing food scraps in the bucket, pressing the air out of them. (A dinner plate works well for this purpose.) Sprinkle in the food scraps with inoculated bran. After each addition of food scraps and bran, make sure to close the lid. Unlike all other forms of composting, air is the enemy with Bokashi. Every few days, you have to draw off the leachate (the liquid created from composting) using the spigot or pouring from the lower bucket. The liquid will smell a little sour and sweet, like fermenting vegetables. Because you control the microorganisms, you should not have the foul odors associated with natural anaerobic decomposition. If you are doing it right, you should not be able to smell anything when the lid is closed and only a mild pickle odor when the lid is open.

Bokashi composters are at home in a kitchen and have no odor with the lid on.

This Bokashi bucket has sat for over a month and although food scraps are visible, they have changed during fermentation.

EFFECTIVE MICROORGANISMS

Three types of microorganisms in the store-bought Bokashi bran form the "dream team" to transform your food scraps into an anaerobically decomposed, pickley smelling masterpiece. They are lactic acid, yeast, and phototrophic bacteria.

If you start making your own Bokashi bran, you can still buy bottles of effective microorganisms online. These organisms are mixed with the bran and then dried. Once they come in contact with the wet food scraps, they come alive and get to work. Sometimes you have to draw the line and decide that the DIY version is more work than just buying it from the professionals. Similar to donuts, sweaters, and cat food, Bokashi bran exists behind the line that my DIY drive refuses to cross. Should you want to venture into that world, I hear you can learn how to do anything on the Internet.

After a few weeks, the food scraps still look recognizable, but they have fundamentally changed. The material is now pickled and called "precompost." We will go over a few ways to use this material at the end of this section both for those with a backyard and those without a backyard.

You might be thinking, why would I use Bokashi if I have a backyard bin? Valid question. One reason might be that you find going out to your compost bin every day or every other day too much of a chore and would rather only do it once a month. Bokashi would also be useful if you are using a community garden compost bin and want to accumulate food scraps in your home for a few weeks. Another reason: you can compost small amounts of meat and dairy using Bokashi. The acidic fermentation kills pathogens, opening up your list of compostable possibilities. Or maybe you just really like the smell of pickles and want to keep an interesting conversation starter in your kitchen for when guests come over.

One word of caution: If the bran does not work or the food scraps have too much air, Bokashi can transform into a rather disgusting mess that will turn the stomach of even the stoutest person. Bokashi is not for everyone, but if you believe the benefits outweigh the risks, give Bokashi a chance. You may help push this fringe practice into mainstream composting.

BOKASHI BUCKET

IIIIIIIIIIIIIIIIIIIIIIIIIIIIIIII

Any buckets that nest in one another will work for this project. If you are fortunate enough to have feline housemates, you may have more of the notorious yellow kitty litter buckets than you know what to do with. As a last resort, you could also just purchase 5 gallon (19-L) buckets from the hardware store.

If you are going all-in on this method, create two of these Bokashi systems so one can be finishing while you add to the other.

MATERIALS NEEDED:
- 2 buckets
- Drill with ¼-inch (6-mm) drill bit
- Cloth rag
- Scissors

SPACE NEEDED: 18 × 18 inches (45 × 45 cm)
TIME NEEDED: Less than 1 hour

LET'S DO IT

STEP 1. You have two buckets; one will be the inside bucket and the other will be the outside bucket. Drill lots of holes (twenty-five to thirty at least) in the bottom of the inside bucket.

STEP 2. Now, cut a rag into the shape and size of the bottom of your bucket and place the rag at the bottom of the bucket. This rag will allow liquid through but will keep small bits of food out of the bottom of the bucket, making your "Bokashi tea" harvesting cleaner. Alternatively, you could use an old window screen of the same size.

STEP 3. Nest your holey bucket inside the non-holey bucket. Remember, we are trying to create an environment with as little air as possible, so really push those buckets together. You want about a 2-inch (5-cm) gap between the bottom bucket and top bucket on the inside so the liquid can go through those holes and have a space to collect.

Drill about twenty-five holes in the bottom of the bucket, allowing leachate to leave the top bucket into the bottom.

To store the Bokashi composter in your kitchen, you could snazz up the buckets with some paint. The buckets I acquired were black plastic and I felt like they would blend into the background nicely and maybe a little more elegantly than the white plastic. Of course, I probably spend way more time thinking about composting buckets than your average friend.

Tightly nest the two buckets together to create an airtight system.

Add 1 cup (50 g) of Bokashi bran to add special microorganisms and start your system.

Now that you have your Bokashi setup, you can start Bokashi composting. I recommend starting first with purchased Bokashi bran. You can buy a supply that will last you several months online. Here are the steps for filling your Bokashi bucket:

STEP 1. Put down your circular rag in the bottom of the holey bucket.

STEP 2. Sprinkle the inside of the holey bucket with a handful of Bokashi bran (about 1 cup [50 g]).

STEP 3. Put in your food scraps. Only do this once a day or, better yet, every other day. You want no more than a 2 inch (5-cm) layer.

STEP 4. Add two handfuls of Bokashi bran to cover.

STEP 5. Push out the air using a plate or something similar.

Add food scraps only once per day or every other day to limit exposure to air.

STEP 1. Every other day, drain off the excess liquid by pulling the buckets apart and emptying the bottom bucket.

STEP 2. Once the bucket is full, leave it undisturbed for 2 to 3 weeks to finish fermenting. Don't panic if a white mold appears; it won't hurt your Bokashi.

Use a plate, newspaper, or other similar covering to push out air from your Bokashi system and cover the food scraps.

Liquid from your Bokashi setup makes a powerful fertilizer. Dilute 1 tablespoon (15 ml) per gallon (3.8 L) of water.

BRIGHT IDEA

The liquid you pull off the Bokashi, sometimes called Bokashi tea, can be a very strong fertilizer full of beneficial microorganisms. Dilute this liquid at least 100 to 1 with water and use it to water your plants. You can add about 1 tablespoon (15 ml) to 1 gallon (3.8 L) of water. The liquid is very acidic and will kill your plants if you do not dilute. I'm not saying I know this from experience or anything.

USING YOUR BOKASHI COMPOST

You can use Bokashi in a few ways: finish composting in a traditional backyard composter, dig into your garden, or use in a container for planting. If you have a backyard composter, this is the best option because the Bokashi compost will quickly finish decomposing in that environment. The bran will also add beneficial microorganisms to your compost. Win, win.

If you chose the bin route, bury the food scraps, just as you would the fresh variety, under a nice layer of leaves. These fermented food scraps break down faster than fresh food scraps added to your backyard bin. Although the Bokashi compost is acidic, the bin seems to balance out and not have any problem adjusting.

If you dig your Bokashi composting into the garden, dig a 12-inch (30-cm) trench. Dump in the Bokashi composting, and completely cover with the soil you removed. Let the Bokashi compost sit for at least 2 weeks before planting anything in that area. The material needs to finish decomposing and is still too acidic to come into contact with plant roots. You'll know it is ready when you dig into the soil and your food scraps have disappeared.

When using in a planting pot, fill the pot with one-third potting soil and one-third Bokashi compost. Mix those two layers together well and then cover with one-third potting soil. Again, wait 2 to 3 weeks before planting.

Do not add already moldy food scraps to your Bokashi system. The mold on them could outcompete your microorganisms in the bran and mess up your system.

Chopping up the materials to small sizes before adding to the Bokashi bucket will increase your chances of success. Larger pieces of food ferment more slowly and can add unwanted air pockets to the bucket.

Bokashi Compostables

WHAT TO ADD
Fresh fruit peels and cores
Fresh vegetable scraps
Small leaves from houseplants
Cooked vegetables and grains
Small amounts of meat and small bones
Small amounts of dairy
Coffee grounds and tea leaves

WHAT TO AVOID
Already moldy or slimy food scraps
Yard trimmings
Animal manure
Large food scraps

Bury your Bokashi precompost under a layer of leaves just as you would fresh food scraps. You will notice the Bokashi precompost breaks down much faster.

Composting Pet Manure in Your Backyard

WASTE FROM MAN'S BEST FRIEND

Ah, dog poop. Our furry friends bring so much love and joy into our lives, but they have this one downside that no one likes to deal with. It is smelly and, depending on the size of your dog, can add up to quite a large amount of waste. According to the U.S. Environmental Protection Agency, the average dog excretes ¾ pound (340 g) of poop a day or 274 pounds (125 kg) per year. Wowza, Fido! In this section we will discuss two methods for safely managing your dog's poop in your own backyard.

DOG POOP CAN MAKE YOU SICK

First, I will attempt to scare you from adding dog poop to your regular backyard compost bin. It is a really bad idea. Dog poop contains pathogens that can make you and your family sick. Unless your pile gets up to a consistent 145°F (63°C) throughout the pile for 3 days, you are not guaranteed to kill all of the pathogens. Professional composters usually need waste from twenty dogs to create a large enough hot compost pile to make this happen. If you have this many dogs and want to try a hot composting method, do some research—but for the rest of the 99 percent of dog owners without their own giant pack of dogs, we will focus on more practical methods.

What's the big deal with pathogens, you might ask? A study in Northern Italy found multiple strains of bacteria in dog poop left on the streets that was resistant to antibiotics. Some antibiotic-resistant strains found can cause urinary tract infections, meningitis, bone and joint infections, and boils. Researchers also found giardia, a microscopic parasite that causes a diarrheal illness known as giardiasis, which I am sure is as fun as it sounds.

If you tried to compost dog poop in a regular composter and it didn't get hot enough, you could be spreading pathogens into your garden from your finished compost. As my mom would say, better safe than sorry.

Hildi is not surprised that the average dog creates 274 pounds (125 kg) of manure per year.

Guy's pack of three will not create enough waste to heat up a hot composting pile.

OTHER PET AND ANIMAL MANURE

If you are lucky enough to have herbivore friends in your life, such as hamsters, gerbils, or rabbits, you can and should compost their manure and bedding with your regular composting methods. That stuff is compost-making gold. The urine and manure contain high amounts of nitrogen ready to decompose and the bedding offers a perfect balance of carbon broken down into small pieces. You do not need to treat herbivore manures with either of the methods in this chapter.

Should you have a snake, ferret, bearded dragon, or some other carnivore, you could use the methods described in this chapter as long as the manure isn't mixed with bedding.

Although CJ is adorable, his poop contains pathogens and must be handled carefully.

WHY DOG POOP CAUSES A PROBLEM IN THE ENVIRONMENT

Dog poop can make you sick, and it also can cause environmental issues in two ways. It can decompose and add too many nutrients to the water when it washes into our waterways. This can cause algal blooms, making the water green, murky, and smelly. The pathogens on the poop can also wash into the waterway. Too much poop can actually make the stream, river, or lake unfishable or unswimmable.

METHODS YOU CAN USE

Now that I've totally bummed you out with the pathogen/parasite/environmental disaster talk, let's get back to the positive. Dog poop does contain quite a bit of nitrogen and other nutrients that are good for the soil. And human ingenuity has made it possible to safely manage the dog poop in our own backyards.

Dog owners report one perhaps unexpected benefit when handling their dog poop with one of these methods—their regular trash doesn't smell nearly as bad as it used to smell.

Solar Digester
Solar digesters use the heat from the sun to decompose food scraps and dog poop into nutrients that migrate into the surrounding soil. The material decomposes so completely that you don't actually harvest any compost. Every few years you may have to scoop out a few shovels of really tough residue left behind.

They may resemble their traditional composter cousins, but solar digesters have a few features that set them apart. First, a basket-like container buried under the ground gives the material direct access into the surrounding earth from all sides but above. Next, the cone-shaped container above the ground is double-walled, which helps trap heat and really cook the materials inside.

This solar digester keeps a pretty low profile in a mulched garden bed.

Installation Steps and Tips

When installing a solar digester, you need to dig down deep enough so the basket can live underground. Test the drainage of your soil by pouring a bucket of water into your freshly dug hole. If it sits there for more than 15 minutes without draining, you need to dig a little deeper and install a layer of equal parts gravel and soil under the basket.

Snap the basket onto the inside layer cone and place it into the ground. Snap the outer layer on top.

Fill in the soil surrounding the basket and bury the top cone part a few inches (5 to 7.5 cm).

The model I purchased included a special enzyme to get the digester started, but you don't have to continuously add the enzyme.

Solar digesters allow you to compost dog poop and food scraps, including meat and dairy. Do not, however, add any yard trimmings to your solar digester as it will clog up the digester and keep it from working properly. You also may need to slow down in the winter.

Dig down several feet to fit the basket underground.

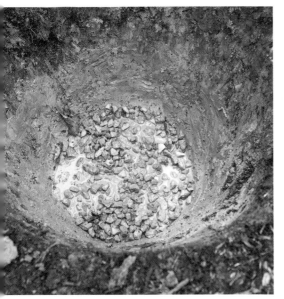

The heavy clay soil of our installation site drained very slowly, so we added a layer of mixed gravel and soil under the basket.

The underground basket of the solar digester is ready to accept food scraps and dog manure.

DOGGY BAGS

I'm not talking about the kind you bring home from a restaurant with your leftover goodies, but the kind you use to pick up your dog's droppings. These will likely not decompose in either method explained here, even if they claim to be "biodegradable." You can try it, but you risk having to remove the bags later on, or worse, clogging up the system so it doesn't work. Better to toss those bags in the trash.

HERE, KITTY

Why not give our little feline friends some attention and compost their manure too? Well, cat poop comes with a whole host of separate issues, including the toxoplasma parasite that can harm human fetuses. You also have to deal with the cat litter that would clog up either system listed in this book, even the pine nugget–type litter. Technically, if the cat poop was completely separated from the litter and not handled by a pregnant woman, you could use these methods.

◀ Sorry, kitty, you may be adorable, but your poop can contain pathogens.

UNDERGROUND TANK WITH ENZYMES

This method is similar to the solar digester, but it uses more enzymes and less solar power to liquefy the dog manure. Septic systems are commonly used to deal with human waste, and we can employ the same concept on a smaller scale. First, you bury a vessel in the ground. In our case, a 5 gallon (19-L) bucket should be able to handle one dog's poop. If you have large dogs, you could also use a small trash can. You can purchase septic tank enzymes at your local home improvement store. The enzymes "attack" the poop and turn it into a liquid that will seep into the surrounding soil safely.

You can purchase doggy septic systems relatively inexpensively online if you desire. Some have nifty foot pedal–lifting lids and other features that our bucket DIY may not have. Know, regardless, that you are still dealing with dog poop and thus, it will smell when you open the lid. However, you should not be able to smell anything when the lid is shut.

▶ Bailey loves the doggie septic system that will liquefy his manure and provide nutrients to surrounding plants.

Important winter note: Once your outside air temperature goes below 40°F (4°C), the septic system will slow down and no longer work as well. I recommend that you stop adding the dog poop in the winter and resume again in the spring.

This system makes sense if you have a fenced-in yard where your dog "does its business." Use a poop-scooping tool and deposit the poop into the bucket. If your dog goes on walks and you transport your dog poo in bags, empty the bags into the septic system and throw away the plastic in the trash.

Enzymes and water in the underground tank dissolve the dog manure into nutrients for the surrounding soil.

COMPOSTING PET MANURE IN YOUR BACKYARD

PET SEPTIC BUCKET

||||||||||||||||||||||||||||||||||||||

Location matters! Be sure your pet septic is out of the way and not close to a stream or other natural waterway. You also want it to have good drainage and be close to a hose (if possible). Choose an area surrounded by dirt or mulch rather than grass. Placing this in your grassy yard just means you have to mow around it and that could add unnecessary stress to your life.

MATERIALS NEEDED

- 5-gallon (19-l) bucket
- Drill
- Shovel
- Septic enzymes

SPACE NEEDED: Less than 2 × 2 feet (60 × 60 cm)

TIME NEEDED: 1 hour

LET'S DO IT

STEP 1. Drill lots of holes in your bucket both in the bottom and the sides. I would recommend at least twenty to thirty holes. No need to measure or make pretty starburst patterns here. This is a bucket you bury in the ground to decompose your dog's poop.

STEP 2. Find a location in your yard that is out of the way, not close to a stream or pond, and with good drainage. Dig a hole deep enough for your bucket. To test the drainage, pour water into the hole. If after 15 minutes that water is still sitting there, you need to add a layer of gravel under your bucket.

Ivy approves of her new DIY pet septic hidden behind a shrub.

Drill at least twenty to thirty holes to allow access to the surrounding soil.

STEP 3. Place the bucket in the ground. Add a little septic enzyme powder and add your dog poop. Add enzymes about once per week. Once or twice per week, fill your septic system up with water. This is easiest if you can reach your water hose to the system, but you can also carry a bucket of water over.

OPTIONAL: Label the top of your bucket so unsuspecting friends walking around your yard know what they are getting into if they lift the lid.

Dig a hole deep enough to fit the bucket in an out-of-the-way location.

Sprinkle septic enzymes in your system once per week.

Harvesting and Using Your Finished Compost

|||||||||||||||||||||||||||||||||||||||||

ALL GOOD THINGS COME TO THOSE WHO WAIT

After a few months (or a few weeks for you hot composters), you will inevitably want to harvest your brown gold. We could become philosophical and say that composting, like life, is more about the journey and not the destination and that your months of work tending to your compost pile, adding food scraps and leaves, checking moisture levels, and aerating when needed were the true joys of a backyard composter. But that would be absurd.

You would not make a delicious batch of chocolate chip cookies and then refuse to eat at least one. Although we enjoy all the steps of composting, harvesting your finished compost takes the cake as the best day in a composter's life. At least the composting part of your life (we are not that sad). Digging into the compost pile to reveal crumbly dark brown humus with a sweet, earthy scent may be more satisfying than eating a warm cookie right out of the oven. Maybe.

ARE WE THERE YET?

Deciding when your compost has finished decomposition does not require a degree in soil science. If the material is not steaming and no longer resembles the original banana peel, you can call it finished. Some fragments of partially decomposed wood and other tough fibers hang on, but they add a nice texture to the compost that most plants will appreciate.

With several composting methods, such as a compost tumbler, the material leaving the bin may not have entered the final, longer stage of decomposition. No need to worry. This material will continue to decompose after you use it in your garden.

Expect to harvest compost from a traditional contained backyard unit once or twice per year. Typically, I harvest my compost in the fall to make room for the influx of leaves. I will harvest small amounts again in the spring for new beds or to help seedlings. The average backyard

This finished compost is ready to harvest with only a few eggshells left undecomposed.

The average compost bin will create about one wheelbarrow full of compost a year. Sit back and admire your beautiful compost harvest.

compost pile or bin will create one heaping wheelbarrow full of compost a year. It provides enough to spread a ½-inch (1-cm) layer over about 300 square feet (28 sq m).

If you use the hot composting method, you could harvest compost every few months, but this method takes a level of time and dedication most composters, myself included, do not have. Tumblers also generate finished compost faster than other methods, so expect to create finished compost every few months with a tumbler as well.

Harvesting Compost from a Single-Bin Unit

Single-unit composters win the crown as the most common type of backyard composting. If you only have one backyard compost bin, you will need to follow a few special steps to harvest the material because you continually add food scraps on top of the finished compost. You can follow these steps for a leaf bin or any single-unit model.

STEP 1.   First, jiggle your compost bin and try to lift it off your pile. If it just won't move, start into step 2 until you can lift it up and out of the way. Shoveling from the side of an exposed pile offers much better ergonomics than shoveling out of the top of the bin. After you lift the bin off, the compost inside holds its shape like you were molding a sandcastle on the beach.

STEP 2. Remove any unfinished material from the top of the pile. Shovel (or pitchfork) the material into 5-gallon (19-L) buckets or a wheelbarrow. This step is the least fun of the whole process because this material can be partially rotted and usually contains a fair number of squiggly decomposers. If the thought of seeing maggots eating your food grosses you out (no problem, I don't judge), freeze your food scraps and do not add them to your compost bin for a few weeks before harvest. Also, consider implementing the two-bin system in the next section.

STEP 3. Once you have cleared away the food scraps and undecomposed material, you will hit the brown gold. Shovel the treasure into a wheelbarrow and admire. Keep an eye out for large sticks or pieces that have not quite finished decomposing and pull them out of the finished compost.

STEP 4. After harvesting all the finished compost, put the bin back in place and restart your pile with the scraps you removed in step 2 and the pieces you pulled out while harvesting. Bury any food scraps with leaves.

Lift a single bin off of the compost pile before you harvest to make removing the unfinished material easier.

BRIGHT IDEA

Move your compost bin to a different area of the yard every time you harvest. The rich, crumbly soil left under a compost bin provides the perfect spot for some lucky new shrub, tree, or bed of plants.

If you purchased a plastic compost bin, you may have a little access door in the bottom of your bin that the manufacturer intended for harvesting. In my experience, this little door does not make harvesting easier. Sometimes, if you need just a few shovels of compost, you can open this door and pull out what you need. However, when you want to harvest a whole compost bin full of material, trying to dig all the material out of this door feels like trying to move a mountain with a spoon. Moving the whole bin out of your way to expose the compost proves much more efficient.

THE MORE THE MERRIER: WHY YOU MAY WANT TWO BINS

Maintaining two compost bins provides many benefits if you can afford the space in your yard. If you have two bins, you can fill one up and allow the materials to compost while you add to the second unit. You still need to aerate and check the moisture level of the first bin, but when harvest time comes around, you have a full bin of finished compost that requires little to no sorting.

Create a two-bin system simply by purchasing two compost bins instead of one. Or when you build a DIY bin, construct two instead of one. If the thought of shoveling squishy old melons full of maggots makes you scrunch your nose, I highly recommend the two-bin method. You can appreciate your macroinvertebrate friends from a distance without feeling the need to strike up a conversation.

Some sophisticated gardeners may even have three-bin composting units. They add materials to one unit and have the material in the second and third units at varying stages of decomposition. If you have a very large garden and need to process a great deal of material, consider a three-unit compost system. Harvesting material from a three-bin unit only requires pulling finished material from the oldest pile.

HARVESTING COMPOST FROM A TUMBLER

Unless your model of compost tumbler has two compartments, you will face an issue similar to single-unit composters: the need to separate unfinished compost from finished. Use the tumbler's fast composting to your advantage and do not add compostables for 3 to 4 weeks before harvesting. You could freeze these food scraps (label the containers well or your family may create smoothies from less-than-desirable scraps) and set aside yard trimmings for that period.

Harvesting finished compost from a two- or three-unit composter is easier than harvesting a single bin. Each unit can hold compostable materials at different stages.

Freeze your food scraps for a few weeks before you harvest your compost tumbler. It will make harvesting easier and set you up with a nice volume of scraps for the next batch.

Finished compost from a tumbler will smell sweet and earthy and no longer resemble the original material, except for sticks and other woody debris. Shovel the material out of the tumbler and into a wheelbarrow or bucket. Compost from a tumbler will continue to mature after you integrate the material into your garden.

THE LIFE—CHANGING EXPERIENCE OF SCREENING COMPOST

I never used to screen my harvested compost. It seemed like a waste of time when I could simply shovel out the finished compost and spread it around my garden. Why mess with an extra step?

Most composting is a waiting game. You spend months adding food scraps, leaves, and other material to the bin, turning the pile, and checking the moisture level. But when the process is complete, you have the satisfaction of pulling out shovelfuls of brown gold. Screening elevates that satisfaction to a whole new level, transforming your backyard compost into something you would pay top dollar for at a garden store, only better, because this compost is your creation.

You just have to experience the feeling for yourself. Sometimes I will stand back with a satisfied grin just admiring my full wheelbarrow of beautiful, dark-brown crumbly goodness. Feel proud. You made this compost out of what some people consider to be garbage.

Sometimes specialty garden stores will sell compost screens, and you can find a few outlets online. Compost screens resemble the devices old-fashioned miners used when panning for gold, only our gold filters through, leaving the undecomposed bits on top. The easiest-to-use compost screens stretch across a wheelbarrow so your finished compost filters directly into the wheelbarrow. Screen with ½-inch (1-cm) holes provides large enough openings for compost to sift down while still screening material out. Smaller mesh will suffice but may require more work to push the desired material through.

Screening compost requires only three easy steps:

STEP 1. Place your screener over a wheelbarrow or bucket.

STEP 2. Plop a shovelful of compost on top and move the material back and forth. I prefer to do this with gloved hands so I can rescue any worms from the compost screen guillotine.

STEP 3. Throw anything too large to go through the screen back into the compost pile for further decomposition.

A compost screener fits across a wheelbarrow and creates beautiful finished compost.

Working material back and forth over a compost screen allows you to save worms and pull out large items that are not quite composted

Help your garden thrive by supplementing your soil with compost.

Screening compost proves easiest with relatively dry compost rather than mushy and mud-like compost. If you have compost on the squishier side, consider setting it out on the ground or a tarp to dry for a day. Drier compost will clump less and break apart easily as you screen.

Unless you practice incredible meticulousness when adding materials, you may encounter non-organic items as you screen your compost. These could include plastic identification tags from plants, pantyhose used to tie staked tomatoes, produce stickers, or the occasional random toy (if you have kids like mine). Pull these out and reuse or throw away as desired.

The Toughest Compostables

Most materials added to your compost will end up indistinguishable from each other. The banana peel and apple core look identical when decomposed. Some of our compostables, however, possess a stubborn streak, and we will find them in finished compost.

Eggshells are the most obvious material in screened compost. These usually break into tiny bits but decompose slowly, resulting in finished compost with many shards of eggshell. If this look bothers you, you have two options. First, simply don't compost eggshells. Second, grind the eggshells up into a powder. As you can imagine, grinding eggshells is a time-intensive activity requiring you to dirty up a blender or other chopping device.

I kind of like the look and know a secret benefit of eggshells in your compost when used as mulch: supposedly, eggshells deter slugs because the shards slice at the slugs' bellies when they come to enjoy your plants. While this might seem like a cruel and unusual form of torture, anyone working to eliminate pests without using pesticides should appreciate the value of deterring slugs.

Other compostables you will find as you screen include mango seeds, avocado pits, shells from nuts, and tough, woody debris. Toss these back into your bin to continue decomposing. If you do not screen and they end up integrated in your garden, they will just finish their decomposition in place.

USING YOUR FINISHED COMPOST

Now that you have harvested your treasure, you have the fun of deciding how to use it. Unless you composted with an integrated method that left the compost in place, you can cart your compost anywhere in your garden. I spread the love around when I use compost, but your needs may differ from mine.

Consider all the areas in your garden. Do you have any underperforming beds that could use a little lift? Is your grass a little patchy or discolored and in need of some fertilizer? Are some of your beds lacking a fresh coating of mulch? The answers to these questions will lead you to some uses over others.

Mulch for Beds

Finished compost, particularly if you took the time to screen the compost, works well as a mulch in garden beds. You may discover that you want to display your prized creation in the most visible beds in your garden. Simply sprinkle the screened compost around plants as you would hardwood mulch.

This application mirrors what happens to decomposing material in nature. When plants and animals die in a forest (or desert, or prairie, or ocean), they decompose on the ground and then become the top layer of the forest floor (or whatever habitat in which they happen to die). Worms, other decomposers, and rainwater pull the nutrients down into the earth. This natural humus layer builds up over time.

A few inches of finished screened compost will beautify your garden, amend the soil, and provide shade for the soil underneath. Applying compost in this way helps the soil underneath retain water and maintain a healthy and diverse profile of soil life. If mulching around trees or shrubs, leave a few inches of gap between the compost and the bark so you do not start composting the tree.

Amending Soil

When you have a new garden bed or very poor soil, working the compost down into the soil will help improve the humus and topsoil layers, drainage, and nutrient availability. Amending soil with compost looks like you would imagine. Dump some compost on top of the soil and work it in with a shovel (or tiller if you have one). Amend the soil when the ground is not too wet or too dry and you will save your back muscles the extra work.

As you integrate the compost into the soil, remember that plants need the minerals from the soil as well. Planting straight into compost rarely works. Generally, you want to add 2 to 4 inches (5 to 10 cm) of compost for every 6 inches (15 cm) of soil. Use your judgment based on the quality of your soil and how much compost you have to go around.

These peonies love their new topdressing. The compost will add nutrients to and protect the soil underneath.

Mix one part compost to two parts potting soil when using compost with potted plants.

Make Potted Plants Happier

You can also make use of your compost in potted plants, both indoors and outdoors. In a more compact space, you will want to ensure that the ratio of compost to potting soil is more exact than when you amend soil on the ground. Too much compost in a pot could burn the roots or kill the plant. But the right amount of compost in a pot will give you the most amazing patio tomatoes you have ever seen.

When potting plants, you want to mix one part compost to every two parts potting soil. Mix the two materials together before adding the plant to the pot. Water the plant well and relax. Depending on the type of plant you potted, the compost may provide the plant with all the fertilizer it needs.

If the plant is indoors, you may want to pasteurize the soil to avoid any diseases to which indoor plants are more susceptible. To pasteurize the soil, simply sprinkle the soil on a baking pan and place it in a 200°F (93°C) oven for 1 hour. Allow to cool before you plant your indoor plants.

Seed Starter

Many gardeners want to provide their most delicate plants, otherwise known as seedlings, the benefit of finished compost. Aside from amending the soil, you can use a mixture of finished compost and vermiculite to cover seeds after you plant them. Vermiculite adds lightness to the compost that allows small seedlings to push through to the surface.

Mix compost and vermiculite in equal parts and spread it over seeds at the depth required for that plant.

Lawns Want Compost Too

Sometimes your lawn needs a boost or all you have is a lawn with no garden beds. You can use compost to fertilize your lawn and amend the often-neglected soil underneath.

As a topdressing, compost will work its way between the blades and amend the soil supporting your grass. Screened compost works best because it has a fine texture. Dry compost will also distribute more easily into the grass. Simply spread about ¼ inch (6 mm) of fine-textured compost across the lawn. Use a leaf rake or a push broom (talk about raising your neighbors' eyebrows) to work the compost into the blades. Water your lawn to further encourage the compost to dissolve and amend the soil. Wait a week to mow, giving gravity time to pull the compost down into the soil.

If you want to overachieve, consider aerating your lawn before you apply the compost. Many home improvement stores will rent a core aerator to punch 2- to 3-inch (5- to 7.5-cm) holes throughout your lawn. These holes provide air and nutrients to the roots of your lawn. If you aerate before applying the compost, the compost will find its way into those holes and down into the soil to amend it more easily.

Growing Mushrooms in Compost

Delicious fresh mushrooms are one of my top-five favorite foods. Just thinking of perfectly sautéed baby portabellas with golden brown edges in a buttery sauce makes my mouth water. When I learned that people actually grow their own mushrooms at home, I felt like a whole new world opened up to me. You too can grow edible, delicious mushrooms at home; many mushroom varieties love to grow in crumbly, moist compost.

I once took a class on growing your own mushrooms, and one quote from the speaker stuck with me: "All mushrooms are edible at least once." You have to be very careful, because some mushrooms possess chemicals creating psychedelic effects that could cause permanent brain damage, and other varieties could kill you.

But we are not talking about foraging the forest for mushrooms. We are talking about gardening your own mushrooms in a contained environment using finished compost and purchased spores. You need to take a few basic precautions when using compost and growing your own mushrooms. First, you need to find a source of mushroom spores. Several companies online sell these, and I would strongly recommend going with a reputable company and not borrowing spores from your hippie neighbor who spends a little too much time in his basement.

Most reputable sources of spores can tell you which mushrooms are easier to grow and which like compost as a growing medium. Oyster, button, and shiitake all seem to grow easily for beginners, but button mushrooms prefer compost over other mediums. When you purchase mushroom spawn, you receive a mixture of mushroom spores (the microscopic cells responsible for spreading the fungus) and the ingredients the mushrooms need to thrive.

Aside from a reputable source for your mushroom spawn, follow all of the spore source's suggestions for preparing the compost so you do not accidently cultivate a fungus existing in the compost and eat the wrong mushroom. Some serious mushroom growers create a specialized compost just for growing the type of mushroom they desire.

Spreading about 2 inches (5 cm) of compost on an existing raised bed will help supplement your soil and make your garden greener.

Raised Beds Love Compost

Whether you have existing raised beds to amend or you plan to construct new raised beds, your finished compost has your back. For an existing raised bed, spread about 2 inches (5 cm) of compost over the bed in the fall and then cover it with mulch. The mulch and the compost will protect the soil over the winter. You can also amend the soil in the spring with finished compost as a layer on top for the no-till method or worked into the soil.

Constructing a new raised bed will use more compost. Most experienced gardeners recommend a mix of 60 percent topsoil, 30 percent compost, and 10 percent potting mix. Thoroughly mixing these three materials before planting should provide a nice starting material for your plants. Raised beds, though often open at the bottom, follow similar rules as potting plants with compost. Add the compost carefully to make sure you do not add so much that you deprive your plants of the important minerals in soil.

BREWING COMPOST TEA

Often, we wish the benefits of our compost could stretch farther across our gardens. If you find yourself looking around feeling like you have more plants in need of compost than you have compost, consider following a tip from serious composters: brew some compost tea. Compost tea transforms compost into a liquid fertilizer, spreading the compost love to more of your plants. It provides soluble nitrogen and beneficial microorganisms to your plants immediately, and the process, while more complicated than applying compost as a soil amendment, is easier than brewing your own beer.

When you make compost tea, you encourage the beneficial bacteria living in your compost to multiply like crazy over a short period of time. Plants love these bacteria, so providing a

Strawberries love compost whether grown in containers, compost socks, or garden beds.

Growing strawberries in a compost sock has been shown to reduce root rot.

Many plants like compost, but none are quite as red, sweet, and tempting as strawberries. Strawberries need well-drained soil in which to grow, or they could face black root rot. Compost offers the perfect solution, providing an ideal growing medium for the little red fruits. Many gardeners plant strawberries in mounds or in raised beds because they like well-drained soil. Incorporate at least 2 inches (5 cm) of compost in the top 6 inches (15 cm) of soil.

Some gardeners even create compost "tubes" or "socks" using cotton or burlap mesh to grow strawberries. You can purchase compost socks or make your own. Fill an 8-inch (20-cm)-diameter tube with compost. Make the tube as long as you need, but most are between 3 and 6 feet (90 cm to 1.8 m) long. Lay it on top of the soil and slit the tube every 8 inches (20 cm) to plant a strawberry plant in each slit. Install a drip irrigation system nearby and watch the strawberries thrive. The USDA has shown that compost socks significantly reduce the occurrence of black root rot and increase fruit yields 16 to 32 fold.

boost of the bacteria to your plants will help them absorb more nutrients. The combination of the sugar in the molasses and the aeration from the aquarium pump help fuel the explosion of beneficial bacteria.

You must use completely decomposed compost when making the compost tea, or you could end up with some weird fermented food scrap moonshine not fit for drinking or applying to plants. Many vermicomposters choose this method because vermicomposting results in a relatively small quantity of finished compost compared to backyard composting. Most compost tea brewers use found or pieced-together setups with a hodgepodge of materials that look less than impressive but work just as well as the fancy sets available online.

COMPOST TEA

||||||||||||||||||||||||||||||||||||||

I am certain I do not need to say this, but as a disclaimer, do not drink this tea. Even with 2 tablespoons of molasses, it will taste like dirt. Literally. Brewing compost tea requires only a few basic materials and takes less than a day. The resulting liquid acts like a fertilizer for your plants.

MATERIALS NEEDED:

▸ 5-gallon (19-l) bucket or old plastic cat litter bucket

▸ Approximately 4 to 5 cups of finished compost (about one shovelful)

▸ Pantyhose (creates a "tea bag" for the compost)

▸ 2 tablespoons (30 ml) sulfur-free molasses

▸ Aquarium pump

▸ Watering can

SPACE NEEDED: 1 × 1 foot (30 × 30 cm)
TIME NEEDED: 24 hours

LET'S DO IT

STEP 1. First, fill the bucket within a few inches (5 to 7.5 cm) of the top with water. If the water is chlorinated, give it a few hours for the chlorine to evaporate.

STEP 2. Place the finished compost into the pantyhose and push it down to the toe area. The pantyhose acts as a bag to hold the compost but still allows water to penetrate, just like a tea bag.

STEP 3. Place the compost tea bag into the water.

STEP 4. Add about 2 tablespoons (30 ml) of molasses to the bucket and stir.

STEP 5. Place the aerating part of the aquarium pump into the bucket and weight it down with rocks if necessary. Turn on the pump.

STEP 6. Give the compost tea about 24 hours to brew.

STEP 7. You should see a frothy top on the compost tea 24 hours later. Pour the mixture into a watering can and dilute it 1:1 with dechlorinated water, if desired.

Brewing compost tea creates a powerful fertilizer so you can spread your compost love even further around your garden.

If you do not have an aquarium pump, you can remove the pantyhose and mix the compost every 20 minutes for 3 hours. A garden stake or other long tool works well for this purpose. Your goal in stirring is to completely aerate the liquid, so do not hold back in your aggressive stirring. Honestly, aquarium pumps are cheap, so unless some hands-on repetitive stirring sounds like fun to you, I recommend throwing $10 down on an aquarium pump. You can also omit the molasses in the recipe and still end up with some nice compost tea.

After you have made the tea, you can use the leftover material in the pantyhose as a soil amendment to add humus material to your garden. To scale up this process and brew a large amount of compost tea, you could use a garbage can or a 30-gallon (114-L) plastic drum and increase the recipe accordingly. If you do scale up, consider how you will remove the compost tea from the container. A spout or spigot near the bottom of the container will allow you to fill up a watering can. Place the spout at least 6 inches (15 cm) from the bottom so any settling compost does not clog up the drain.

|||||||||||||||||||||||||||||||||||||||||

OBSESSED YET?

Even before you harvest your first shovelful of beautiful, crumbly compost, you may develop an obsession with composting. It is hard not to fall in love with an activity that improves your soil, benefits the environment, saves you money, and gets you outside. If you are not already, you will be scolding your spouse for throwing out a banana peel or inventing new ways to steal your neighbor's brown paper bag of leaves.

If you have a deep desire to learn more about backyard composting, I highly recommend you check to see if a nearby garden center or local government office offers a Master Composter class in your area. These intensive classes cover many topics you already learned in this book. They also offer hands-on demonstrations and supply you with a network of people in your area who are as crazy about composting as you are. Also, when was the last time you could call yourself a master of anything?

So many people tell me in the hushed tone of a confession that they actually like composting more than they like gardening. I feel the same way. Composting is so practical and useful. You take your leftovers and give back to the soil, replicating nature. Once you have a feeling for balancing the browns and the greens, memorize your list of acceptable and unacceptable materials, and work aerating and watering the pile into your routine, composting becomes second nature. It is hard to imagine a time when I routinely threw away those banana peels and coffee grounds.

I hope this book has provided you the inspiration and knowledge you need to start successfully composting in your own home or backyard. Rest assured, composting has a forgiving nature, and no matter how many mistakes you make along the way, compost happens. The materials you add will decompose and turn into a valuable soil amendment in the end. Happy composting!

BIBLIOGRAPHY AND REFERENCE LIST

BOOKS

Appelhof, Mary. *Worms Eat My Garbage.* Kalamazoo, MI: Flower Press, 1997.

Balz, Michelle. *Composting for a New Generation.* Minneapolis, MN: Quarto Publishing Group, 2018.

BioCycle. *The BioCycle Guide to the Art and Science of Composting.* Emmaus, PA: The JG Press, 1991.

Campbell, Stu. *Let It Rot! The Gardener's Guide to Composting.* Pownal, VT: Storey Communications, 1998.

Gilliard, Spring. *Diary of a Compost Hotline Operator.* Cabriola Island, BC: New Society Publishers, 2003.

Jenkins, Joseph C. *The Humanure Handbook: A Guide to Composting Human Manure.* Joseph Jenkins Inc. and Chelsea Green Publishing, 2005.

McDowell, C. Forrest, and Tricia Clark-McDowell. *Home Composting Made Easy.* Eugene, OR: Cortesia Press, 1998.

Minnich, Jerry, and Marjorie Hunt. *The Rodale Guide to Composting.* Emmaus, PA: Rodale Press, 1979.

Overgaard, Karen, and Tony Novembre. *The Composting Cookbook.* Toronto: Greenline Products, 2002.

Pleasant, Barbara, and Deborah L. Martin. *The Complete Compost Gardening Guide.* North Adams, MA: Storey Publishing, 2008.

JOURNALS, MAGAZINES, AND ELECTRONIC RESOURCES

Arsenault, Chris. "Only 60 Years of Farming Left If Soil Degradation Continues." *Scientific American* (2017). www.scientificamerican.com/article/only-60-years-of-farming-left-if-soil-degradation-continues

Bokashi Living. bokashiliving.com

Cinquepalmi, Vittoria, Rosa Monno, Luciana Fumarola, Gianpiero Ventrella, Carla Calia, Maria Fiorella Greco, Danila de Vito, and Leonardo Soleo. "Environmental Contamination by Dog's Faeces: A Public Health Problem?" *International Journal of Environmental Research and Public Health* (2013). www.ncbi.nlm.nih.gov/pmc/articles/PMC3564131

"Compost Fundamentals, Compost Benefits and Uses." Washington State University, Whatcom County Extension. whatcom.wsu.edu/ag/compost/fundamentals/benefits_benefits.htm

Cornell Waste Management Institute. Cornell University. www.cwmi.css.cornell.edu/chapter3.pdf

Dickson, Nancy, Thomas Richard, and Robert Kozlowski. *Composting to Reduce the Waste Stream: A Guide to Small-Scale Food and Yard Waste Composting.* Northeast Regional Agricultural Engineering Service, 1991. ecommons.cornell.edu/handle/1813/44736

Doggy Dooley. doggiedooley.com

EcoRich LLC. www.ecorichenv.com/home-composter

Eliades, Angelo. "Deep Green Permaculture." deepgreenpermaculture.com/diy-instructions/hot-compost-composting-in-18-days

Funt, Richard C., and Jane Martin. "Black Walnut Toxicity to Plants, Humans, and Horses." Ohio State University Extension (2015). www.berkeley.ext.wvu.edu/r/download/211509

Green Cone USA. www.greenconeusa.com/green-cone-solar-food-waste-digester.html

Hamilton County Recycling and Solid Waste District. *Confessions of a Composter* (blog). www.confessionsofacomposter.blogspot.com

Hamilton County Soil and Water Conservation District. *2010 Compost Data Chart.* www.hcswcd.org/uploads/1/5/4/8/15484824/2010_compost_data_chart_-_2.pdf

Hoitink, Henry A. J., and Ligia Zuniga De Ramos. *Disease Suppression with Compost: History, Principles, and Future.* Ohio Agriculture Research and Development Center, Ohio State University.

"The Many Benefits of Hugelkultur." *Inspiration Green and Permaculture* (October 17, 2013). www.permaculture.co.uk/articles/many-benefits-hugelkultur

Millner, Patricia. "Socking It to Strawberry Root Rot." *Agriculture Research* (September 2007). www.agresearchmag.ars.usda.gov/2007/sep/root

Natural Resources Defense Council and the Ad Council. Save the Food. www.savethefood.com

Platt, Brenda, James McSweeney, and Jenn Davis. *Growing Local Fertility: A Guide to Community Composting.* Highfields Center for Composting and the Institute for Local Self-Reliance (April 2014). www.ilsr.org/wp-content/uploads/2014/07/growing-local-fertility.pdf

Project Groundwork, Metropolitan Sewer District of Greater Cincinnati. www.projectgroundwork.org

Rowell, Brent, and Robert Hadad. "Organic Manures and Fertilizers for Vegetable Crops." University of Kentucky Department of Horticulture (2017).

Schwartz, Judith D. "Soil as Carbon Storehouse: New Weapon in Climate Fight?" *Yale Environment 360* (March 4, 2014). www.e360.yale.edu/features/soil_as_carbon_storehouse_new_weapon_in_climate_fight

Trautmann, Nancy. "Invertebrates of the Compost Pile." Cornell Composting Science and Engineering (1996). www.compost.css.cornell.edu/invertebrates.html

University of Illinois Extension. "History of Composting." *Composting for the Homeowner* (blog) (2017). web.extension.illinois.edu/homecompost/history.cfm

US Composting Council. *Compost and Its Benefits.* (2008). www.compostingcouncil.org/wp/wp-content/uploads/2015/06/compost-and-its-benefitsupdated2015.pdf

US Department of Agriculture. *Composting Dog Waste.* (2005). www.nrcs.usda.gov/Internet/FSE_DOCUMENTS/nrcs142p2_035763.pdf

US Environmental Protection Agency. "Advancing Sustainable Materials Management: Facts and Figures." (2013). www.epa.gov/smm/advancing-sustainable-materials-management-facts-and-figures-report

———. "Municipal Solid Waste Generation, Recycling, and Disposal in the United States: Facts and Figures for 2012." www.epa.gov/sites/production/files/2015-09/documents/2012_msw_fs.pdf

———. "Overview of Greenhouse Gases." (2017). www.epa.gov/ghgemissions/overview-greenhouse-gases

Waltz, Clint, and Becky Griffin. "Grasscycling: Let the Clippings Fall Where They May." University of Georgia Cooperative Extension (June 18, 2013). www.extension.uga.edu/publications/detail.cfm?number=C1031

ACKNOWLEDGMENTS

Many people helped pull this book together and I hope to capture everyone. First and fore-most, I have to thank my husband, Adam, who provided expertise and creativity in building most of the compost bins you see in this book. Without his knowledge, you would have seen a lot more duct tape. Adam also helped behind the scenes, digging holes, stacking logs, carrying pallets, and reviewing the DIY text to make sure everyone else could understand what I was thinking. My children, Ben and Emily, were true sports, tagging along on photo shoots, eating too many frozen pizza dinners, and leaving mommy alone to write. I'm surely the luckiest lady alive to have such a supportive family.

Many friends and family stepped up to be models, including Jane Allan, Akiko and Imu Aloway, Adam Balz, Benjamin and Emily Balz, Charles Robert Balz Jr. (Uncle Charlie), Christo-pher Balz, Josephine Balz, Lois Borich, David Daniels, Julie Drábková, Bill Felix, Kelly Fogwell, Gretchen and Brude Fortin, Jacqueline Green, Brian and Lucy Howe, Kathy Kugler, Carol Lawson, Alice and Bill MacFarland, Brad Miller, Matthew and Iris Peterson, Charlene Schell, and Dorothy Wilson. You were all so generous with your time and patient with my some-times-bonkers instructions ("Now hold the food scraps like you are about to drop them but don't actually drop . . . ."). And last, but certainly not least, many thanks to all of the adorable dog models, including Bailey, CJ, Guy, Gypsy, Hildi, Ivy, and Wesley.

I have so much gratitude to my family, friends, and friends of friends who let us build com-post bins at your homes and who were not also models thanked above, including George and Joy Balz, Jeff Caywood and Rob Neal, Mary Rita Dominic and Buddy Goose, Bryan Griffin and Tim Schraw, Elizabeth and Justin Ogilby, and Elizabeth J. Winters Waite. A big thanks to Build-ing Value and the Civic Garden Center of Greater Cincinnati for hosting our photo sessions as well. And a special thank you to my late friend John Barlage, whose pickle-barrel connections are still helping me out.

What you read in this book draws on the collective knowledge of hundreds of other gar-deners and composters from books, articles, and websites listed in the references but also from very helpful social media groups. Hugelkultur Gardening, Cincinnati Permaculture Guild Forum, Home Composting, Greater Cincinnati Gardening Club, and others answered my questions and offered suggestions. How amazing that I can connect with and learn from peo-ple around the world from the comfort of my couch.

I am forever grateful to my friends who tested all of the crazy composting methods I con-cocted, including Jane Allan, Gary Dangel, Hannah Lubbers, Kat McLane, and Dorothy Wilson. I'm also grateful to my many other friends who offered to test a method, but I was too dis-organized to pull one together for you. And I would be remiss if I did not thank my mom, Sharon Brotherton, for introducing me to composting when I was a child.

Of course, a big thank you to Andrea MacFarland for spending so many Saturdays (during a pandemic, no less) photographing compost bin construction, food scraps, worms, and dog-gies. You even braved your fear of chickens and entered the coop to snap photos. I appreciated making this book with a great friend who also happens to be a talented photographer. Your beautiful photos bring the projects and composting to life.

ABOUT THE AUTHOR

Michelle Balz is a longtime backyard composter with a passion for reducing our impact on the planet. Her first book on backyard composting, *Composting for a New Generation*, was published in 2018. In addition to teaching hundreds of classes on composting, she has reached many more people through the *Confessions of a Composter* blog. Since 2002, Michelle has worked as a solid waste (garbage) professional, encouraging residents and businesses to reduce their waste and use fewer resources. She has a bachelor's degree in environmental studies and a master's degree in professional writing, both from the University of Cincinnati. You can follow Michelle on Twitter and Instagram under the handle *compostgeek*. Michelle lives in Cincinnati, Ohio, with her high-school-sweetheart-turned-husband Adam and two adorable children, Benjamin and Emily.

INDEX